The Seeker

The Seeker

Phil Morimitsu

**ILLUMINATED WAY
PUBLISHING, INC.**
PO BOX 27088
GOLDEN VALLEY, MN
55427-0088

The Seeker

Copyright © 1992 Phil Morimitsu and Coleen Morimitsu

All rights reserved. No part of this book may be reproduced, stored in a retrieval system, or transmitted in any form by any means, whether electronic, mechanical, photocopying, recording, or otherwise without prior written permission of ECKANKAR. The terms ECKANKAR, ECK, EK, MAHANTA, SOUL TRAVEL, and VAIRAGI, among others, are trademarks of ECKANKAR, P.O. Box 27300, Minneapolis, MN 55427 U.S.A.

Printed in U.S.A.
Library of Congress Catalog Card Number: 92-71541

Edited by Joan Klemp
Anthony Moore
Mary Carroll Moore

Cover design by Lois Stanfield
Cover illustration by Neil Massy
Back cover photo by Bree Renz

To all my teachers

Contents

Preface ix
1. The Mtsham 1
2. A Link with Infinity 5
3. The Old Monk's Story 13
4. I Leave Thung-yule 19
5. The Naljorpa 23
6. Katsupari 29
7. Kotan Runa 35
8. The Records of the Kros 43
9. The Kadath Inscriptions 47
10. Reflections 55
11. The Council 61
12. Banished 67
13. Lo-tsa-ba and Shen 73
14. The Eyes of a Small Animal 79
15. The Harvest 85
16. The Tax Collector 89
17. Judged 93
18. Sold as a Slave 101

19. The Bandit	107
20. Ge-sar	113
21. Rol-pa'i	119
22. A Lost Love	125
23. Katmandu	129
24. Zoji La	133
25. The Return	141
26. The Old Man	145
27. The Gatekeeper	149
28. Agam Des	153
29. The Cup	159
30. Stranglehold	163
31. I Face My Past	165
32. The Greatest Power	169
33. The Beginning	173

Preface

Have you ever tried to find something without any clues, directions, or someone to help you? At best, it can be difficult. At worst, impossible.

Even when we've found something precious—a moment of extreme peace, a feeling of at-one-ment with all life, the love of a dear one—it can be lost in a flash, leaving you wondering if it was ever real; often leaving you with the sick feeling that you may never find it again.

This book is based on a past-life memory from Tibet in the 1600s. As a monk, I searched for something that I've searched for in this present life as well. Though I now have a guide, as I did in that lifetime, I was not always able to hear or follow directions clearly, mostly due to stubbornly held opinions. In dangerous territory, that can lead to painful or even fatal incidents, and while doing research for this book, I had several painful and close calls. All of this pointed out to me the wisdom of Santayana's quote, "Those who cannot remember the past are condemned to repeat it."

In my case, I realized this applied to my own personal history through many incarnations, and the repetition of the same mistakes.

Writing the book and having to face in this lifetime many of the same tests and obstacles as in that life in Tibet has not been easy. At times, it was frustrating and disillusioning.

There is one thing I did learn, though. And like so many lessons from Divine Spirit, it wasn't at all what I expected or even wanted to learn. It's this: If you have the right teacher or guide and the persistence to learn to listen and trust, your teacher will help you overcome foolishness, inaccuracies, and vanity.

So what does that leave you for entertainment? Not much, materially—but it does leave you with what really matters in life. It leaves you with what I've lost more times than I care to admit. And it leaves you with what I once found in old Tibet, as the seeker.

1
The Mtsham

"You are the youngest to have ever entered the *mtsham,* Denpei Ranshin. Are you prepared?" the old lama asked me as I stood in his dimly lit chamber.

"I am ready!" I replied. I knew that I would be sealed in the meditation cave with water and food lowered to me through a shaft.

Stroking the gray and white stubble on his chin, he rocked gently from side to side.

"What will you attempt to accomplish while in the mtsham?"

"The consciousness of God!" I stated flatly.

He ceased swaying, and his eyes widened in mock awe.

"Ahh—So you would enter the mtsham to gain the consciousness of God? A worthy goal, indeed!" he said in a patronizing voice. I was not used to being treated this way by him. I began to defend myself, but he raised a single finger, stopping me.

"You cannot attain God Consciousness—if there *is* such a thing—until you first have silence in your beingness. And silence cannot live in you as long as noise is your guest," he whispered.

He no longer mocked me, but his words still stung. Silence? During my entire youth, I had uttered hardly a sound except when spoken to. I looked to him in protest, but he cut me short once more.

"*True* silence, Denpei—*true* silence! Even an ox can keep its mouth shut and say nothing. But only a trained being knows true silence. If a man were never to utter a word amongst his fellowmen, yet babbled in his mind, would he have true silence? No! When you enter the mtsham seeking the consciousness of God, seek silence first, for silence will introduce you to God." He closed his eyes and nodded curtly, signaling that our meeting had ended.

Bowing, I left my teacher's chamber confused, but only for a moment. Outside the door were Tangri and two assistants, waiting to lead me to the mtsham. The two monks quickly got up from the ground where they sat, brushing the dust from their hands. Tangri was leaning against the wall, arms folded, with a look of disdain for me. My stomach tightened, and my fists clenched at the sight of these three. Tangri pushed himself languidly from the wall and, without a word, walked away. One of the monks jabbed my side, motioning for me to follow Tangri. I glared at the monk. He returned a toothy grin but backed away, not wishing to start a fight.

Tangri was slightly older than I and much larger. Always ambitious, he was quick to fulfill the head lama's requests when there was advantage to be gained for himself. He combined any authority he gained with his size and sheer force to keep the rest of the novitiates under his rule. Periodically, he would bully the younger, smaller monks until their will broke and they cowered at his sight. We had fought many times. While

I was seldom victorious, I would not back down. Now he kept his distance unless in the company of his allies. Tangri reserved a special hatred for me.

A few steps from the mtsham, I felt the air quicken. Instinctively, I braced myself for danger, but it was too late. In an instant, the two monks following me had pinned my arms behind my back. Tangri turned slowly, his eyes narrowing. When he saw that I was helpless, held by the two monks, a malevolent grin spread across his face. His upper lip quivered. He was clearly savoring this moment.

"Take this into the mtsham with you, Denpei Ranshin!" he said, as he spat on my face. Enraged, I struggled to break free, but the two monks held me fast. Without warning, Tangri slammed his fist into my stomach. I doubled over, choking and fighting for air. My legs buckled; only the two monks held me up. Weakened, but gaining my breath, I looked up, only to see a knee smashing into my face. A dull, cracking thud sent me into the world of blackness.

As the numbing faded and melted into pain, I felt myself dragged, lifted, and finally thrown roughly on a dank, clay-packed floor. Rolling facedown so I would not choke on the blood that ran from my nose, I heard Tangri's gruff orders to the monks as they closed up the opening of the mtsham, shutting away the last of the daylight with a wall of mud bricks. The earthy smell was muted by the icy cold of winter. A thick coat of yak dung was smeared over the cracks in the bricks to seal out all traces of light. The monks worked quickly before the steaming, warm dung froze. With the black isolation came pain from Tangri's blows; and with the pain, I felt a raging anger. It would be three years, three months, and three days before I would again see the rays of the sun.

2
A Link with Infinity

The floor of the rocky, barren, desertlike plain swept up to treeless mountains. Millions of years ago, this plain was the bottom of a great ocean. But now, the north Tibetan plateau was the floor only for thin, crisp air and an icy river which snaked its way through the mountains. At this high altitude, the clarity of the air made distances deceiving. Mountains that seemed close enough to be touched with a finger were, in fact, days' travel away. At night during the dry season, one could see dim stars that could not be seen anywhere else on earth. Meteors streaked like white threads across a blanket of night sky, enlivening the deep evening air every few moments.

The ring of white-capped mountains in the distance circled the flat plain. In the middle of the plain, a single rock formation jutted up, surrounded by a few dozen mud-brick houses. The *gompa,* a whitewashed monastery of one main building and several smaller monks' quarters, perched on the top of this lone jagged rock. The monastery faced the rising sun. On its roof were strings of red and yellow prayer flags and long, bushy bunches of black yak hair tied to poles. They flapped in unison, carrying prayers to the gods through the early-morning wind.

On the monastery roof, two monks clad in maroon robes stood beneath the flags and bunches of yak hair and solemnly blew eight-foot-long horns. The notes echoed off the surrounding mountains like forlorn cows bellowing for a lost calf.

Forty monks huddled in their places, shivering slightly in the frigid air. Younger novitiates opened aged, wooden book covers to yellowed pages. Then the chanting began. Softly at first, but quickly building to a steady din, it was accompanied by the brassy, muted banging of cymbals and the beating of various-sized gongs and bells. The melange of sounds blended to form a lonely drone, an ancient wakening call to the sun.

In the distance, a monk approached the mud wall that sealed the mtsham. Scanning the surface with his hand, he produced a sharp bone from the folds of his robe and began to chip away at the dry, hardened mud. After poking and digging, he produced a smaller, more pointed bone and worked it into the shallow hole he'd made. As the instrument probed deeper, he turned it slower until suddenly it broke through. Withdrawing it carefully, he blew away the dust to examine his efforts. Satisfied, he backed away slowly and returned to the monastery.

The tiny hole the monk had made in the wall would allow the sun's light to enter the cave. Each day, for another three weeks, he would gradually widen the hole, allowing my eyes to slowly become accustomed to daylight, so I would not be blinded by a sudden burst of light.

Inside the mtsham, I had begun to prepare myself for a new life outside the cave. By the time the monks came to open the mtsham, I was strong enough to walk.

Once out of the cave, I was escorted to the living

quarters of the gompa where my skin was cleansed and oiled. The hair that flowed halfway down my back was cut short, then my head was shaved. I was thin, but it would only be a matter of weeks before my body reached full strength again.

In a small, barren room, new clothes had been laid out on a straw sleeping mat. I was much taller now and had long outgrown my chuba, the long maroon robe of my youth. Unable to remain in the stark room any longer than I had to, I changed into my new clothes and climbed to the roof of the main prayer hall, the highest point of the gompa. From there, I could see the entire valley and the surrounding mountains.

The slow, chilly breeze tasted of blue snow and mountaintop ice. The dull snapping of the prayer flags in the wind chanted a random rhythm. Below me, men in maroon chubas scuttled between buildings, unseeing of all the life around them. Perhaps in time, I too, would lose the awe for life, but now my senses were given a feast.

I stood on the roof, entranced, until the shadows of the mountains turned the day's brilliant colors to grays and blacks. Then I gazed at the stars, once again greeting the old, familiar patterns they made, until the cold air began to numb my hands and feet.

The next morning, I heard muted voices and footsteps scraping the gravel outside of my room. It was Tangri, with another massive brute of a youth. He was a *dobdob*—a child left at the gompa by poor parents unable to feed or care for him. Uneducated, and perhaps too coarse to do anything else, these peasant boys were taken into the gompa and cared for in exchange for training as monastery policemen. A dobdob's main function is to scare peace and order into the inhabitants of the gompa.

In the three years I had spent in the mtsham, I had grown considerably. Tangri's size was once imposing, but the difference was not as noticeable now. As we stood before each other, Tangri wore a pugnacious glare that struck me as comical. I had not seen faces for so long; expressions seemed strange masks for what lay inside a man's heart. I returned his look neutrally and sensed that he had been unsure of our relationship, bringing the dobdob as an ally, in case of a fight.

"The head lama is dying. He wishes to see you once more before he leaves this world for the next," Tangri said. He turned his back and walked away. "Follow me," he grumbled as if it were a careless afterthought.

This left the dobdob sneering at me. He stood a full handspan taller than I, and his muscular bulk told that he originally came from the far northwestern provinces of Tibet. His face, blackened and shiny from old yak butter, looked as though it had been burnt in a furnace. His robe, tattered at the shoulders and badly frayed at the bottom, was black and shiny as well, from grease and dirt. He looked as if he had done nothing to better his appearance in years, except that his head was recently shaven. Turning slowly, he sauntered ahead in a vain, syncopated strut, his spine stiff with pride.

Passing through the dark, musty, yet vaguely familiar corridors, we approached the head lama's room. Tangri stood tautly aside, waiting for me to enter. His tension exuded heat and desperation despite the cool sneer on his lips.

The atmosphere changed dramatically as I stepped through the portal. The still, heavy scent of Death hovered patiently, waiting for the lama to give up his last breath.

"Da-lay," the head lama croaked in a hoarse voice.

He was motionless; I thought at first he was part of the mortared walls and inanimate furnishings.

"Da-lay," I returned quietly. My fingers pointed upward, hands together in front of my face in the traditional Tibetan salutation.

The walls of the lama's room were richly painted with mandalas. Bowls of yak-butter candles burned into puddles of filmy ooze, emitting a musky smell that matched their yellow light. The elder monk sat on a red-and-gold cushion, his thick maroon robe wrapped around his shoulders. He was ready to receive Death in the traditional sitting position.

The sight of him brought me great sadness. I remembered him as a strong man with much life in his body—now, he seemed smaller and weaker. His eyes and cheeks were sunken, and the balding head seemed fragile. His countenance, always shining, was now dim; and dustiness seemed to cover his face. Though his voice was a raspy whisper, it was still tempered with kind gentleness.

"You were a boy when we sealed you into the mtsham, the youngest ever to attain the title of lama in this gompa; now you are a man. You have attained the eyes of the wise. Tell me what they have seen to make them so."

I relived the images from the first moments in the mtsham. Once again, I felt the terrible rage for Tangri as I lay helpless on the mtsham floor and the last rays of sunlight were sealed from my eyes.

Pain slowly crept upon my numbed senses, stirring a wrathful fire. Instinctively, my arms pushed my body off the cold ground to burst through the wall before the yak dung had a chance to set and dry. I wanted to fight them all, but my body gave out. Collapsing, I choked for breath and fell into a black unconsciousness.

Did I awaken from the deathlike sleep, or did I remain? My eyes no longer served me—open or closed, they saw only darkness. Did I remember the wounds from Tangri's blows, or did I dream them? They hurt little, compared to the vengeful energy behind them. With each reminder of his hatred, a deafening storm thundered throughout me.

"Om mane padme om," I droned the familiar mantra, attempting to dispel the disruptive images. But the more I chanted, the more it fueled my temper. I had entered the mtsham to gain the consciousness of God, but in reality, I had the consciousness of a madman. I was powerless to control this burning rage with my own will. This only increased my frustration.

Days, weeks, or months passed in this hell. My stomach did not hurt from Tangri's blows but from the gripping tension in my body. Finally, the pain sent me hurtling into an abyss. Sleep, unconsciousness, waking state—all smeared into an indefinable blackness. I fell to the ground, panting and exhausted.

I awoke with my cheek to the cold, damp, clay-packed floor. Opening my eyes and seeing only darkness, I forgot who and where I was. Collecting my memory, I sensed something was different. For the first time since entering the cave, it was quiet.

The stillness of the mtsham revealed how much noise my angry thoughts of Tangri had made.

My ears strained to savor the nothingness. My soft breathing soon filled the air until that which had been barely noticeable was now the loudest sound. I listened to the gentle beating of my heart until it too became loud. Somewhere in the cave, ants traveled steadily in their serious, workmanlike gaits, tumbling grains of loose dirt from the walls as if they were boulders falling from a mountainside.

I came to know that there was no such thing as true silence in the physical world. Nor was there such a thing as total darkness. Hundreds of minute specks of light moved in a river of motion. I followed these lights as far as I could, attempting to trace them to their origin. With these lights came the awareness of gentle inner sounds—sounds I knew were always with me, yet never seemed to have meaning until now. They were as fine as mist from mountain waterfalls, flowing from rocky heights.

I was visited by a single pinpoint of light: brilliant white in the center, tinged with blue. A piercing note, as from a wooden flute, blocked out all other sounds. The flashing light disappeared, but the steady tone lingered for a few moments.

In this strange world of unreality and fleeting memories, this Light and Sound provided my only stability. It was at this time that the opening of the mtsham began.

My attention returned to the present. The old monk patiently awaited my answer.

"The blue-and-white star and the sounds... my path is the one that will lead me to their origin," I answered evenly.

The elder monk drew back and inhaled deeply, making a hissing sound. His eyes glimmered in recognition, and I sensed a tinge of satisfaction.

He nodded his head slowly, sadly, as if he could see the future.

"You have always been the gompa's favorite student, Denpei. Though there are others older and with more years in the lamasery, it is you I had hoped would succeed me as master."

"I am not ungrateful—perhaps I am unworthy," I

began, but was interrupted.

"No—no, if there is an unworthy one, it is I. I can give you nothing more than words for your search. Do not apologize for what you must do, nor have regrets. Truth does not discriminate where it will be found. It is only important that it be found."

Looking down, he grunted gruffly. "Perhaps it is best that you leave the gompa, lest Tangri or you should die. It would not be the first time a monk has suffered a fatal fall from the high monastery stairs," he said, eyeing my face keenly for a reaction.

"When you came to the gompa as a young child, Tangri grew fearful that there would be less love for him, for I had loved him much before you. He did not realize then, nor does he now, that true love is of an endless supply. When you arrived, he began to compete for my love by placing himself where I would take notice and give favor to him. I have always felt only love for you. Because you were able to give without expecting anything in return, love was always available to you. You both needed love—only your methods of attaining it differed."

With these words, the old angers I held for Tangri weakened, and for a moment, I felt understanding and compassion.

The elder monk became silent. He smiled, changing his mood, "Now it is time for me to reveal what I know." He closed his eyes and rocked gently back and forth as he began his tale.

3
The Old Monk's Story

In my youth, my master took me and a small band of seven *trappas,* adult monks, to the northern highlands—past the great lakes at Siling, over the Tanggula mountains into the cold wilds. Our goal was a great monastery in a tropical land where the knowledge of the universe was kept. The story was passed to us by an elder who claimed to have visited this monastery as a young man. He told tales of beings and records of ancient history that few men in Tibet or perhaps even the whole world had ever seen. He revealed the directions to this place by memory, being far too old to show us the way himself.

"Though we departed in the warm months of summer, the mountains were bitter cold at night. We were well-prepared, but soon travel became slower than anticipated. It was not long before the days became cold. The journey began to exact its price when three of our small band entered the next world by way of the snows and treacherous cliffs.

"After four moon cycles of futile searching, we were enveloped in clouds and blizzards so thick that our vision was lost. We clung to each other's chubas and followed the head lama's lead. The cold became increasingly bitter. Many lost fingers and toes, and the only way we knew we were injured was from the spurting of blood as our fingers or toes broke off. An avalanche carried away two more of our party and stranded the rest of us on a cliff. We were surrounded by crevices so deep that we could not hear the bottom as stones dropped into them.

"Our journey was halted on the side of a mountain with three peaks, like fingers on a man's hand. After three, perhaps four, days on a precipice, we finally began to resign ourselves to our earthly ends. Fires would not burn because of the blowing snowstorms and lack of dry materials. Huddling together for warmth and comfort, we prepared for death. It is not an unpleasant way to die—to leave in one's sleep. As others began their final slumber, I too fell asleep and began to dream.

"In the dream world, we were as in the physical—huddling on the edge of a cliff, awaiting our transition to the next world. The snow and fog created a thick wall of white. Suddenly a great wind blew it apart. For a flashing moment, I saw clearly to the other side of the precipice. And there it was."

The old monk stopped here for a moment and opened his eyes, staring straight ahead, as if he were looking at it now. His mouth hung open, awe-struck. He moistened his lips and slowly continued.

"I saw it for only a moment. Resting on the highest peak of the range was a monastery—or so I thought. It was like none I had ever seen. Though made of stone, it sparkled like the sun on dew. There were green trees and plants and birds. I saw no one, but I knew living beings were nearby.

"The wind continued to blow and quickly covered the small gap in the fog and snow that allowed me to see the magnificent building. Then an angel from the monastery came to me as a small white light, like a star with a blue aura. It spoke to me not in words but came as my own inner voice—only gentler, and stronger. It instructed me to lower myself from the cliff. It disappeared, and I awoke to the world of the physical. As I blinked my eyes, the same thing occurred as in my dream. The wind blew away the fog, and I saw the monastery. But it did not sparkle as it had in my dream, nor were there green trees and plants. It was large and rough, covered with drifts of snow.

"In my excitement, I awakened my three companions. I pleaded for them to hasten and look to the other side of the chasm, but when they finally did, it was covered by the fog again. I hurriedly told them of my dream and what I had seen upon awakening. After some argument by one of the trappas who wished to die peacefully, it was decided I would be lowered from the cliff as instructed by the blue-and-white star. Three man-lengths below us was a small ledge. It was a cave entrance leading into the mountain. Eventually, all in the party climbed down. Though we had no material to make torches, we were able to make our way quite well through the darkness. How many days we traveled this cave I cannot say, but when we finally emerged, we were back in a thick fog. Through this fog we made our way as blindly as in the darkness of the cave. Eventually, we found easier ground, and then familiar land.

"It has been many years since that experience. I have never attempted to return to those lands, for I knew it would have meant certain death, and it was not my fate to leave this world in that manner. I never saw the blue-and-white star again nor heard another speak of it until you. Then, I knew I was to pass this tale on to you," he said, almost out of breath. His time on earth was nearing its end.

"Your old name, Denpei Ranshin, the Innocent, no longer fits you. From this day on, you shall be called Lobnear-Wa, the Seeker!"

As I moved closer, he smiled, took my hand, and slipped three small gold coins into my palm. "Please accept these. You will know when to use them." His breathing slowed, and I sensed the life-force gently ebbing from his body, as he prepared for the transition. Sudden emotion overtook me. My mouth quivered uncontrollably as I fought to keep the sobs from escaping.

At this, the old monk's eyes widened, and in a burst of excitement, he stiffened.

"What is this? How dare you! Have you learned nothing from me in all these years? Imbecile! Do not insult me by wetting me with your tears in my last moments. This body is uncomfortable enough as it is. I wish to shed it in peace. Would you be so selfish as to try to keep me here? Would I keep *you* from *your* search for truth? Let me continue mine!" he rasped in a hoarse voice.

My back stiffened from his reprimand. My teacher had barked sense into my head, but it had left him exhausted. Collapsing on his pillow, he breathed hard. A benign smile was on his lips.

"You see? I can no longer teach you properly. This body has no more strength. But no matter, I will soon have another. In the meantime, you will need to find another teacher. I have taken you as far as I can. May you have much happiness and truth in your journey, Lobnear-Wa," he said, giving me one last look of love and affection. I knew these would be his last words.

The old monk's eyes closed, and the once taut wrinkles in his face relaxed. He looked like a newborn babe snuggling into its mother's arms.

His chest moved, each breath becoming a deep sigh of contentment and relief. His eyes opened briefly and, looking upward, were filled with a gaze that one has when meeting a dear friend. His last breath flew away with joyous expectation, and I knew he was free.

The tears flowed from my eyes. Suddenly, I felt very alone.

4
I Leave Thung-yule

I returned to my room for the last time to gather my belongings. Water would not be difficult to find; there were many mountain streams. My yakskin bag filled with rolls of roasted barley flour and yak butter, a wooden bowl, and the three gold coins were my only possessions other than the clothes I wore.

Making my way from the monk's quarters, I passed the main building and descended the stairs carved into the mountainous rock that connected the gompa with the floor of the flatlands. Halfway down, where the steps turned a corner, I stopped. My stomach tingled a heated warning signal: danger lurked around the corner. The stone stairway had no railing, and a slip meant a terrible fall, most likely death. Sensing someone hidden around the corner, I called out, "Pass—I will wait." Moments later, shuffling feet approached me. It was the giant dobdob with Tangri close behind him.

I stepped sideways against the wall, which was the usual courtesy when two individuals met on the narrow steps. But instead of passing, the dobdob suddenly planted his feet firmly in front of me and grabbed my chuba at the shoulders. He meant to throw me off the stairs. In an instinctive movement, I brought my hands up from my sides, between his arms, and flung them outward, slapping his hands away from my shoulders. The quickness of my defense startled the dobdob and sent his arms flailing.

Tangri, who stood behind him, was struck in the face. Futilely waving his arms to keep his balance, he hurtled backward like a featherless bird off the steps to the rocks below.

He fell more than six man-lengths. His body made a dull thud, and skidded, as loose stones and gravel rolled after him. The dobdob and I moved to the edge of the stairs and watched Tangri limply roll to a stop, amid a river of sliding rocks and dust.

"Get help. I will see if he is still alive," I said to the dobdob as he stared dumbly at the fallen body. "Go!" I shouted, waking him from his stupor. Blinking, he began to move slowly up the stairs to summon the other monks.

* * *

"He will live. It will take many moons for him to heal, but he will live," the head physician of the gompa muttered, wiping Tangri's blood off his hands with a dirty rag. "The bones of his chest are broken, as well as his arms. I have pieced his face together, but he will look strange," he said, shaking his head.

I moved closer to Tangri's broken, unconscious body which lay on a wooden table. Most of it was bundled with cloth bandages, the knobby ends of yak bones protruding at odd angles to keep his broken bones set. I gasped when I saw his face. His right cheekbone had been crushed. The physician had removed the loose fragments of bone and sewn his face with black yak hair. It was a mass of crisscross stitching and oozing blood, mixed with ointments.

"If you are leaving, it would be best to go before he regains consciousness," the physician offered. Nodding, I turned and left.

The spring air showed my breath in puffs of blue fog. The thick sheepskin chuba and a pair of padded, calf-high, yak-fur boots protected me from the crisp, biting chill. Using my training in the art of tumo, I could raise my body temperature to keep warm even in extremely cold weather. Yet the mountain passes were too cold and too long in crossing to rely on it solely. I was grateful for the warmth of my clothes.

I knew my search for the Light and Sound would take me into the forbidding mountains of the north. My thoughts returned briefly to the gompa. Was there anything I could have done for Tangri? Whatever I did, I knew he would think only of revenge. There was nothing left for me there. I walked on and did not look back.

5
The Naljorpa

I looked back on the flatlands and shallow lake basins where I had spent the last nine days traveling. The distance passed quickly on the high, flat plateau, but travel would be slower and more difficult once I reached the mountains. The lonely giants seemed to stretch on forever. Like a secret brotherhood, they sat in silence, linked by a shroud of cloudy mystery, appearing to observe me as much as I observed them.

Children wrapped in bundles of brightly colored, dirty clothes played in the dirt roads, signaling the outskirts of a village, Shire Nor.

A small, shaggy black-and-white dog greeted me and followed quietly. When we reached the village market, he left me in favor of the company of three stray dogs, who snarled over bloody fat scraps of a butchered goat tossed alongside the dirt road.

Having spent most of my life in a gompa, the sight of merchants and their wares was new to me. As I observed them, I was often shoved aside by impatient buyers who chose their goods with loud, serious voices and great animation.

Near the end of the market, separated from the squat buildings, was a small, dusty, black tent. A dried yak head was impaled on a pole. On the ground lay heaps of tanned skins, yak horns, bones of various sizes, bushy tufts of hair, and coiled, braided ropes.

"Da-lay!" a voice called to me as I looked over the coarse, black tufts of hair. It came from a small man almost hidden in the folds of his chuba, huddled next to a smoldering fire.

"Da-lay!" I returned the greeting, moving closer to the red-and-black coals that separated us. Behind the thin, gray wall of rising smoke, I saw a round, weathered face, almost completely dwarfed by his floppy maroon hood. The long sleeves of his chuba concealed his hands. As he squatted, the hem of his coat touched the ground, hiding his feet. Keen, shining black eyes stared expressionlessly into mine, blinking yet riveting.

"You are a stranger?" he said, more as a statement than a question.

I nodded once affirmatively.

"You go to the north? To the mountains?" he said again, in the knowing way of his. Again, I nodded.

"You have money?" he continued. This time I did not nod. He did not wait for an answer, but stood up, pushed open the flaps of his tent, and disappeared. A moment later, he reappeared with a large coil of braided yak-hair rope and held it out to me.

He was almost like a child, as he held out the rope. I stared silently at the coil.

"You will need this," he said, nudging it toward me once with an extended arm. I was surprised that the rope was so light, despite the fact that it seemed to be extremely long. As I hefted it, the man smiled with great satisfaction, which lit his face in a pure way.

I did not understand my fascination for this strange merchant's wares, but the image of my old teacher's three gold coins came to mind. Slinging the rope over my shoulder, I reached into the fold of my chuba and produced one of the coins. As I handed it to the little man, he stuck out his tongue, an act of respect in Tibet. Then he smiled and returned to his spot on the ground near the hot coals.

I resumed my journey. The road became less worn as I reached the outskirts of the village that led to the Tanggula mountains. Suddenly, something smacked me hard on the left cheek. Reaching for my stinging face, I pulled away a handful of wet slime.

My eyes darted to the last tent in the village. A man stood there. He appeared to be a beggar, and he was laughing at me.

"Hey, you—fool! You think it is food I want? Take more of mine!" he said as he threw another handful of the gooey slop at me. "You reflect your own feeble desires on me, do you? Bah! I want nothing of you, insolent worm! It is *I* who can do something for *you* this bright, ugly morning."

Cocking his head to one side, he squinted. "A seeker of truth, are you? I can save you your ignorant wanderings, but I am sure you are much too stupid to listen to me."

Black grease and dirt coated his entire body as he sat in a pile of damp yak dung. His hair, matted and caked with dried, greasy mud, hung down past his shoulders. His clothes had rotted until they now appeared to be a part of his filthy skin. Lice crawled freely over his body, and he made no attempt to scratch or acknowledge their presence. On the ground in front of him was a bowl of tsampa, a hot barley cereal. It was green from the mold which grew on it and infested with worms. The sour, putrid smell wafted in my direction. I had seen these strange eccentrics before.

They were *naljorpas*—beings who supposedly attained a sort of perfect serenity. Yet in many cases, they were merely deranged ascetics that enjoyed showing off their mental prowess by upsetting others' thoughts.

Too surprised to say anything, I paused dumbfounded.

"Are you too proud to ask, idiot?" he purred in a sly, mocking voice.

"Then I'll *tell* you what I know. It is easy to see that you're seeking a great spiritual prize. You, who are so innocent and dumb—a yak would know more about such matters. I read your aura and see that it is the Star and Sound you seek, like a puppy following his master off a cliff."

My face flushed with anger that this filthy, psychic eavesdropper would invade my privacy and mock my goals. Before I could retort, he continued.

"How do I know about your precious thoughts of the Blue Star and Sound? Hah! Because at one time, I too followed them! I have been to the top, and also to the bottom. Now, I have transcended both! I have seen what the Great Being has to offer with ITS most holy Light and Sound, and I have survived the ordeal—more fortunate than the others who vainly tried and lost. I know better. I know there is nothing, so it is best to be satisfied with what you are—as I am! You could save yourself the trouble of a long journey. But of course, that would not satisfy your great vanity, nor would I think of depriving myself of watching another fool fall. And fall you will, for there are many who will try to hasten your demise—and relish in it. With every step upward you take, I will be there to stop you and make sure you slide down with the rest of us. I will be in more palatable bodies than this one, but I will be there. I will hasten your demise this very moment!

The sacred place you so hungrily seek is called Katsupari. So go! I will be there waiting for you, for I am you! Look!"

Dipping two fingers into the filthy bowl, he scooped up some rotting tsampa covered with several squirming yellowish-white worms. Watching my expression intently, he raised it to his face and in one sudden motion, jerked his head back and inhaled the dripping tsampa through his nostrils with a loud, slurping noise followed by the smacking of his lips.

"Ha ha! Do I disgust you? Shock you? Well, this is you! These little worms, these parasites are you; and the sooner you accept them, the closer to God you will be! I am a parasite of this village, just as these worms are parasites of my body. What are you but a parasite in the body of God? Do you not live off His benevolence? You are a worm! You are a parasite! You are me! Go, fool! Vain fool! Hah!"

And he began to laugh. It was a terrible laugh, mocking and hollow. The whites of his eyes showed, making him look like a dead man come back to life. I stood transfixed, watching him indulge in hideous joy as he scooped the rotting, wormy food to fling in my direction.

"Come! Why don't you strike me? Are you too proud to stoop and strike me? Then go, fool! But think on this; you may believe you are too good to strike me. But when you walk away from here, you will carry the desire to destroy me. You will not do so, only because you are a coward and hypocrite! You do not even know it, but you too have been infested with parasites. As I have swallowed the worm, you have just now swallowed me! I live in your body in the form of vanity and anger; and the more you try to destroy me, the more you will feed me! Ha ha!"

I turned to walk away from this madman, burning with the desire to smite him. He screamed after me, "You have not seen the last of me! I shall remind you that I feed on your life-force each time you feed your anger and vanity!"

As I strode purposefully away, the naljorpa broke his laughter and spoke in a softer, malevolent voice, just loud enough for me to hear, "You want God for selfish reasons, and for that, you are the worst parasite of us all!"

These last words made me whirl and shout, "You lie!!" But he was gone. My anger was replaced by confusion, and in the pit of my stomach, I suddenly felt very weak and drained.

6
Katsupari

The howling wind cursed the warmth in my blood, roaring darkness and anger through every valley and crevice in the mountain range. Wind-whipped snow blotted out all vision of the vertical, jagged mountain walls and turned the world a dull grayish-white. It was as if this land desired all living things dead.

Inching along a ledge no wider than a handspan had to be done by touch, for every attempt to open my eyes caused tears to freeze as they formed. Each breath brought terrible pain from the moment the air froze the hairs of my nostrils into sharp needles. The feeling in my toes had disappeared long ago, and I struggled to keep sensation in my limbs. My knuckles had turned a blackish-purple, and my fingers were covered with frozen blood from clinging to the cold, razor-sharp rocks. The wind tore through my chuba as if I were naked. My knowledge of tumo helped little, for I had never before experienced cold such as this.

I had found the three-fingered mountain peaks the old monk spoke of and had gone as far as I could—but now there was no more ledge. I had no strength to return the way I came. A thousand man-lengths stretched between myself and the bottom of the deep ravine. I tied the yak-hair rope around my waist and lashed myself to the rock wall to prevent a fall, but I was fooling myself. While I could not consciously admit it, I knew eventually I would freeze to death. There would be little pain by then, for my body was being numbed by the cold. I buried my face as deeply as I could in the collar of my chuba to allow myself the comfort of some warm air.

The moment I closed my eyes, the blue-white star flashed. An inner voice spoke to my heart, not in words, but in a knowingness, "A few more moments—hold on."

My body shook involuntarily—a feeble attempt to fight off the cold.

The wind slashed its way through the canyon in a fearful attempt to deliver the death blow, but in doing so, tore the veil of cloud and snow.

For an instant, I saw the other side. There stood the monastery the old monk had spoken of. The clouds quickly covered my view but not before I was able to see how near the other side was. My yak rope just might reach. Untying it from around my body with slow, numbed hands, I fastened it to one of the jagged rock spurs—one that moments before had cut my hands. I heaved the coiled rope to the other side, but the wind caught and threw it back. Pulling it up, I tied a rock to the end and tried again. This time, as rock and rope disappeared through the white curtain of wind and snow, I heard it strike the other side with a hollow "clack," then fall into the canyon. Heartened, I continued trying, and on the fourth throw, the rock lodged on the other side.

After pulling it taut and resecuring it, I wrapped

my arms and legs around the horizontal rope. I hung upside down and made my way across the chasm.

* * *

Have I entered the next world? I wondered as I struggled to open my eyes. It was apparent that I was still of this world—pain dogged my senses like a shadow, but at least I was warm now. The corners of my eyes were cracked and bleeding from the ordeal, and I fought the stinging to look at my new surroundings.

Sunlight from a large window reflected brightly off whitewashed walls. I was in a bed, my hands and feet bandaged and treated with herbs and ointments. Next to me, a bowl of water and a candle rested on a small, red-lacquered table. An attempt to lift my head exhausted me, and I lost consciousness again, drifting into dark oblivion.

The falling stopped. The darkness faded as a gentle hand nudged my shoulders, awakening me to the dream world.

My eyes opened to see a young man in a calf-length maroon robe which shimmered with a thousand lights. Shiny black, shoulder-length hair framed his fair-featured face. He was a beautiful being, with high cheekbones and a wide mouth that turned a benevolent smile. Though he looked no more than twenty-five, he possessed a grace that only many years could instill. His eyes were soft, trusting and inviting black pools. As he knelt on one knee in the soft moss where I lay, he spoke.

"We do not get many visitors the way you have come."

"Where am I?" I asked. Wherever I was, I no longer felt pain. There were no wounds, no bandages on my hands. A fine white robe clothed my body instead of the tattered and bloody maroon chuba.

"You are at the Katsupari Monastery!" the young man said with a lilting laugh. "My name is Garlung."

"I am Lobnear-Wa of Thung-yule."

"Yes," the young man answered quietly, with a knowing smile.

"Why is there no pain? Am I dreaming?" I questioned in semi-disbelief.

"Yes, you are dreaming. That is why your body does not hurt, but you *are* at the monastery. You crossed the gorge, and soon after, your physical body collapsed into unconsciousness. We had watched you for a long time and were able to help you only when you made it to our side. Your physical body is being nursed back to health in the monastery and will be unconscious for a time. For now, we meet in the Nuri Sarup, the dream body.

"Katsupari exists at a vibratory rate between the Astral, or dream, world and the Physical. It exists in the Physical as a real and solid monastery, but there are distinct differences. In the Physical, it is coarser. It blends with the mountains and snow, and no man is able to see the monastery unless we allow it. In the Astral, it appears with more vibrancy, and the climate is much gentler. Come, let me show you the grounds!" he said, offering me a hand.

The grounds were not large, for they rested on a series of terraced peaks, but how beautiful they were! Nestled in a tropical garden of palm trees, beds of flowers glowed with color. Long-tailed blue and green birds sang and flew from one palm to another in small flocks. Orange and yellow butterflies floated graciously between flowers, sipping nectar from white-and-pink blossoms of hanging vines. Small animals hopped before us, tamed by the gentleness of the land. Trees were laden with hanging fruits of brilliant colors. Huge yellow, black, and orange-colored fish cruised effortlessly in the ponds and streams that wound their way through the gardens.

Above them loomed the huge monastery; it was like none I had ever seen before.

We walked a white-pebbled path through the lush gardens to the temple's stairs. In front stood an archway three man-lengths high. As we approached, two heavy wooden doors with polished brass rings swung open silently. Inside, all was lit by a soft bluish white glow, as if the walls had a hidden light source. The ceilings were as high as the treetops. In one great hall, large windows revealed a view that extended for many days' worth of traveling over the mountains. Long maroon curtains ran the width of the windows and cascaded to highly polished, light-gray floors. Many visitors were being escorted in and out of the room by attendants in shimmering maroon robes similar to Garlung's.

"There are classes for those who desire the knowledge of the Light and Sound of God, given by Sri Fubbi Quantz, a Master of the Vairagi who is the abbot of Katsupari. The monastery also houses several libraries, such as the Naacal Records.

"The visitors are here by special invitation, and they can only attend in the dream state. Those you see in the maroon robes are chelas, students of the Master, escorting visitors to different lecture halls," Garlung explained.

As we watched the passing crowds of men and women, a collective stirring riveted everyone's attention on one man. He walked from one of the rooms adjoining the main hall. Hundreds of eyes focused upon him as he made his way toward us. I couldn't place it, but there was a strange familiarity about him. With each step he took closer to us, a strange anticipation washed over my body in waves.

The man was nearly as tall as I am and wore a white, shimmering robe. His white hair flowed to his shoulders, and his short beard came to a point on his chin. As he approached, he placed his hands together, fingers upwards, and bowed slightly, Tibetan-style. Reciprocating, I studied his face. He was darker than I, perhaps from the lands to the south, from India. His eyes were like Garlung's—large, deep, dark pools.

"We are pleased to have you with us, Lobnear-Wa," he said in perfect Tibetan. "I trust your stay will be one of fulfillment."

His words were simple, yet his look was one of recognition. His eyes said he knew and understood me—perhaps better than I knew myself. Though I had nothing to hide, it was disturbing that another could see me so clearly. I remembered the naljorpa, and how easily he had read my deepest thoughts. This being, however, was different. As sharp and penetrating as his stare was, I felt myself wanting to trust him. Yet I resisted.

While I stood transfixed in confusion, he put his hands together, bowed, and left us. I saw the loving admiration Garlung had for this man.

Garlung eventually spoke. "That," he said with weighted words, "is the abbot of the monastery, Sri Fubbi Quantz."

The words meant nothing to me, but they sent a shiver up my spine and across my shoulders. The Sound in my inner ears hissed and rang in a high pitch. I wondered if this was the Master I searched for.

7

Kotan Runa

Brilliant whiteness warmed my face. I sensed a tingling in my hands as I sluggishly awoke. I struggled for memory, while my eyes darted for clues of where I was. My attention shot to the doorway; someone was about to enter.

A large man wearing one of the temple's maroon robes appeared. He was two or three hand spans taller and thicker in body than me. Though he moved just a few steps, he revealed the physical mastery of an athlete. A great strength emanated from him, and I sensed he was well aware of this power.

Startled, I sat up from the sleeping mat. I had never seen a man such as this before. His hair was pale yellow; his skin was white. His eyes, instead of the almond shape which was common to me, were rounded and the color of the cloudless sky. I thought he was one of the walking dead or very old perhaps, because of his whitish hair. But he looked far too young to be old, and too alive to be dead.

"You are looking well. That is good," he said in a deep voice that showed a genuine pleasure in my recovery. He must have sensed my apprehension, for he kept his distance in the doorway.

"I am Kotan Runa. I am charged with nursing you back to health. You are strong and have survived when a lesser man would have perished."

"Have I been unconscious?" I asked.

"Four, perhaps five days," he said.

I tried to get up. Our eyes locked intensely, as his deep, expressionless stare challenged me. Suddenly, needlelike bolts of pain gripped my head. Blackness momentarily covered my sight. I fell weakly back on the bed.

The stranger laughed in a soft voice, "Do not struggle; you still need much rest. The bandages from your hands were removed only this morning. You may feel them tingle or itch, but in time they should heal completely."

He made a motion as if to leave, then paused. With a proud grin, he held a fist to his chest and said, "I am of the ancient Uighur race, from the east."

I had been curious as to where he was from but had not asked aloud. Somehow, he had read my mind. His eyes were now sly and sent me the unspoken message: I can hear every thought you have. Do not attempt to fool me, lest you become the only fool.

As Kotan Runa smiled and spoke, a cordial social mask covered what I had just seen and heard, and the gripping pain left my head. "I am pleased to see you are conscious and recovering. I will allow you more rest. When you feel strong enough, simply call for me and I will show you more of the temple. I am at your service!" Bowing, he left the room.

The next day was the first I was able to consciously observe the care given my physical body. Maroon-robe-clad men and women of various races shuttled in, changing my bandages. I was given herbal remedies and nourished with strange, but pleasant-tasting foods and liquids that invigorated me even as they were put in my mouth. I took care to guard my mind and emotions, in an effort to retain my inner privacy.

Days later, I felt strong enough to explore the physical side of the temple and thought to call Kotan Runa. Uncannily, he appeared outside of my door.

"You are feeling well enough to walk?" he asked, laughing, amused by the startled look in my eyes. It could have been mere coincidence that he appeared at my door just as I thought of him, but I knew not to underestimate his abilities.

"Yes, I can walk now," I replied, gingerly moving my legs off the bedding mat. As he helped me stand, his brow furrowed and his voice became solemn.

"You are fortunate, Lobnear-Wa. I have been given permission by the abbot to reveal the Naacal Records to you."

I struggled woodenly to my feet. He assisted by lifting me under my arms.

"The Naacal Records. Garlung mentioned them to me," I said, breathing hard from my efforts.

At the mention of Garlung's name, there was a brief stutter in Kotan Runa's movement as he lifted me; it was nearly undetectable, yet unmistakable. After helping me stand, he forced a smile to hide his uncertainty. I cautioned myself not to think of the break in his consciousness, for I knew he was watching my thoughts. I felt a connection between my guarded feelings and Kotan Runa's reaction to the mere mention of Garlung's name. It was fear.

As we walked to the opposite end of the temple, Kotan Runa pointed out various inscriptions and paintings on the walls. It was a welcome diversion.

The physical temple took longer to walk through than the astral temple, but it seemed smaller, less expansive. It was clean, yet there was a hardness that the temple of the dream state did not have. It lacked a certain magic.

Kotan Runa stopped at the entrance to one of the larger rooms. "The library of the Naacals," he said with veneration, extending an open palm, welcoming me.

The room was more of a wide hallway. A floor-to-ceiling window at the far end illuminated the high walls with a view of the endless snowcapped mountain range. Cold, crisp air chilled my legs as we entered. The library revealed thousands of stone blocks neatly organized on wooden shelves extending to the ceiling. A tall, rough, wooden ladder rested against the left wall.

Kotan Runa led me to the right wall and picked a smooth stone from a rack. "These can be scanned or read by touch—either way, it is through the heart that they reveal knowledge," he said, stroking it gently with his fingers.

Handing me the stone, he waved to a row of stone tablets, inviting me to peruse them at my leisure. There were thousands of them, perhaps millions. The face of each small stone was square, polished smooth, with tiny, unfamiliar writing delicately etched, front and back.

Kotan Runa's movements quickened jerkily, as Fubbi Quantz entered the room. It was the first time I had seen the ECK Master in the physical body. A radiant warmth and spontaneous joy emanated from him, similar to that from the head lama at the monastery in Thung-yule.

Kotan Runa bowed reverently and moved aside for the ECK Master. I clasped my hands together and bowed Tibetan-fashion, as did Fubbi Quantz.

He extended his hand, palm upward in a gesture

for me to place the stone I held in his hand. He closed his eyes as he accepted the small, smooth stone, "Place your hand over mine and close your eyes."

I found myself in a dark inner world, holding his hand and the stone.

A gentle warmth surged through me, as if I were in the current of a stream of water. "Listen for the Sound. Look for the Light with your inner eyes," his voice soothed me.

The Blue Star flashed before me. Like a tiny opening of brilliant sunlight, it blinked, then disappeared as quickly as it had come.

A faint tinkling of far-away tiny bells accompanied images of the stones in the room. I was now able to read the previously unfamiliar writing on them. Their words told the story of Katsupari monastery. As I listened, the voice of the stones became my own.

"Many thousands of years ago, from the capital city of Khara Khota, in the great empire of Uighur, came the Living ECK Master of the times, Rama. Exiled from Uighur, he came to Tibet to build a temple—a center of great knowledge and learning with records and libraries of universal truths. Housed in this temple are the Kadath Inscriptions, the history of all the Living ECK Masters in all the universes; and the Records of the Kros, which tell of the history—and future—of the earth planet; and the most valuable of all, the first hadji, or volume, of the Shariyat-Ki-Sugmad. This temple was named Katsupari. The ECK Masters have always guarded it and will continue to do so until the end of time on the earth planet.

"Built with the knowledge of the times, Katsupari continues to grow. The perceptions of its visitors constantly reflect the changes. As man learns and grows, Katsupari grows. As man falls in dark times, its visitors become fewer. Nevertheless, they come here to fulfill the spiritual needs of mankind. At Katsupari, there will always be much which visitors will never understand, nor even perceive. The temple always teaches what is sacred: knowledge and love. When man begins to know and love, he begins his journey home."

The pictures ended, and I was back in the temple, staring at the stone with the strange writing I could no longer read.

"You have learned to read the Naacal records quickly," Fubbi Quantz said gently, "but are there questions?"

"Yes," I asked, "who were the Naacals?"

"The Naacals were a brotherhood of priests on the continent of Mu, many tens of thousands of years ago. They traveled to all parts of the earth to teach the religion of the Ra-Mu and kept excellent records of their motherland and humanity on earth. They were sympathetic to the ECK Masters, for their own teachings were inspired by the ECK. Some assisted Rama in the building of Katsupari and left the monastery one of the few remaining complete sets of records.

"You have learned the secret of reading the Naacal Records, Lobnear-Wa. From this point on, you will have unlimited access to them, as long as your motives are for the service of the whole."

I nodded in recognition. The ECK Master placed his hands together, bowed, and departed.

As he left, I glimpsed a strange image out of the corner of my eye. Turning to look, a cold, terrible shock clutched my insides. Against the wall stood the filthy naljorpa that had mocked me as I left Shire Nor; only now, he seemed to possess more malignant power than before. As his hypnotic eyes bore into me, I saw his face clearly—through the dirt, the right side of his face was bleeding and mangled with yak-hair stitching. It was Tangri. A sneering mask of anger and jealousy branded his blackened face. Fear writhed and crawled through my stomach like worms as I turned to confront him directly. But as I did, the image disappeared. In its place stood Kotan Runa, arms folded, with a keen, penetrating glare aimed at me.

8
The Records of the Kros

For days, troubled memories of the naljorpa and Tangri in Kotan Runa's face left me confused and listless. Was the naljorpa correct in his prophecy? Would he follow me wherever I went, draining me, and feeding on my life-force through fear?

One evening as I lay on the sleeping mat in my quarters, I closed my eyes, searching for answers. In a moment, I was walking up a winding stone staircase with Garlung. A quick smile from him assured me we were in the dream world.

"Garlung, can you tell me more about what you call the ECK?"

We reached the top of the stairs and passed through a sparkling corridor.

"I can teach you what I have learned from Sri Fubbi Quantz. That which empowers all life is the force called the ECK. As the ECK passes through forms, It causes them to vibrate. As the ECK passes through men, It causes a vibration that can be heard, seen, and felt in our inner universe. We can find our way back home to the Creator, SUGMAD, by following this wave of the ECK."

"Can you tell me more of Fubbi Quantz?" I asked.

"He is of the Order of Vairagi. Vairag means detachment, the ability to view life objectively rather than seeing it through eyes influenced by indulgences, prejudice, or opinion. As an ECK Master, he has mastered himself and surrendered to the life-force of the universe, the ECK. He has also earned the title of spiritual respect, *Sri.*"

Determined to find a reason for Kotan Runa's mental probing of my thoughts, I asked, "Can this ECK Master read the thoughts of others?"

"If it were needed, but he never does so without permission. Such an invasion is contrary to spiritual law," Garlung answered.

"Can others in the temple read thoughts?" I asked.

After a slight pause he said, "Perhaps."

"Why does Kotan Runa fear the mention of your name?" I asked pointedly.

Garlung did not react in the same manner as Kotan Runa, but calmly raised one eyebrow and smiled wryly. He stopped at an arched entrance and nodded into the room. "The Records of the Kros. Perhaps you will find your answer there."

It was a massive room, tall as ten men and the size of a small barley field. Smooth, white stone walls and shelves caught sparkling flecks of light. Interspersed between the shelves were thick pillars, also made of the sparkling white stone. Each row of shelves contained many small, wafer-like clear crystal stones. Scanning the neatly arranged rows, my gaze fixed on the waiting figure of Sri Fubbi Quantz standing in one of the aisles. He nodded to Garlung, who bowed and left the room.

Greeting me, Fubbi Quantz spoke softly, "This section of the stones marks approximately the present time on the earth world. Behind it lies the past—ahead of it, the future. Of course, all future events are subject to change. You are welcome to look if you wish."

I reached for a stone from a section in the future. Closing my eyes and feeling the cool, smooth surface, I saw a vision of myself in an unfamiliar land.

I stood on a narrow mountain pass amid a chaotic herd of many yaks and horses. Two other men, one with leather armor and a sword, held the frenzied animals at bay. On our right was the cliff's edge and on our left the unscalable rock wall of a mountain. Behind us, the road was blocked by an avalanche. The road quaked with an ominous thundering.

"Come!" I called, running toward the edge of the cliff.

The two men looked at each other with alarm. "No! I die here fighting!" the armed man shouted, brandishing his sword.

"Come!" I repeated firmly, continuing to the edge of the precipice. "It is our only chance for survival!"

The scene faded, and I found myself returned to the present, in the large room with Sri Fubbi Quantz. Gently removing the stone from my hand, he replaced it on the shelf.

"The real enemy is not what lies over the cliff, nor even the danger approaching you on the road. Those are merely the effects of the true adversary, which is fear," he said.

"What is the meaning of the vision?" I asked.

"The Records of the Kros have given you a gift. You will know what to do when the time comes. But whether or not what you have seen will indeed be a gift depends on the discipline of silence. All events are subject to change. Do you understand?" I did not fully understand the vision, but I sensed the importance of silence in the matter and nodded in agreement.

9
The Kadath Inscriptions

"How are your hands this morning?" Kotan Runa asked briskly.

"They are healing," I replied, examining the delicate new skin. My wounds from the cold and rock cuts were healing quickly.

"Then come. There are many things in the temple for you to see."

I followed him down the hall.

"If you are well enough, there are positions in the temple to fill. You are strong. I have need of one like you to assist me, or," he said, with a calculated pause and a sly grin, implying a hidden meaning behind his words, "if you prefer, there are other positions. It depends on you."

"I would be honored," I returned.

He nodded, assessing me with narrowed eyes. The hall ended with tall, wooden double doors. A monk standing by swung the heavy doors open at Kotan Runa's command, then left us.

"The physical Records of the Kros," Kotan Runa said. He gestured expansively to take in the whole room.

The room was not nearly as large as its dream-world counterpart. Rows of dark, ancient, wooden shelves holding boxes of small stones filled the room.

As I looked, Kotan Runa asked casually, "Garlung has been showing you the temple in the dream world?"

Caution instinctively surrounded my thoughts. I nodded.

"You saw the Records of the Kros last night with Fubbi Quantz? If so, I can allow you to look at the physical records," he added eagerly.

Remembering the vow of silence, I said nothing. Tension mounted with each passing moment. I fought the urge to speak, to give in to his will. Finally, in a controlled, menacing burst, Kotan Runa spat, "Do not play guessing games with me! I know all occurrences within the temple walls. It is my duty! My questions are only to help you, to confirm what I already know."

His anger was a last resort to intimidate me into giving up my will, to make me speak. Standing my ground, I returned his glare. When he realized he would not succeed, he grudgingly drew back his forceful energy.

"Come!" he ordered, as he planted quick, heavy steps down the hallway, not bothering to wait for me. We stopped at a small, curved alcove nearly hidden by shadows. A winding, stone stairway led us below the monastery's main floor. Aromas of cooking food wafted up as we descended into the well-lit kitchen.

Three workers in maroon robes and tan aprons prepared grains in large bowls on a wooden table. Three black brick ovens exuded great heat, causing the air near them to waver. Several wooden tubs for washing food and ceramic pipes for carrying flowing water lined one wall. A large vent near the ceiling funneled in cool air and dispelled the heat generated by the ovens. Large, polished copper pans graced the walls, while blackened kettles dangled over long, wooden tables, smoothed shiny from years of use. The dynamic working bustle of the kitchen made it a cheerful place.

Changing his mood in the presence of the others, Kotan Runa's voice oozed cordiality, "Lobnear-Wa, these are the kitchen workers; Mukanume, Zansar, and, as you probably know from the dream world, Garlung." His voice hardened slightly as he introduced Garlung.

The three interrupted their chores and gathered near. Mukanume appeared to be the eldest. A handsome woman with graying black hair tied in a bun, she bowed and smiled, reflecting a quiet strength. Zansar, a muscular, swarthy man, nodded a jovial greeting. I learned later that Mukanume came from a southern province of China and Zansar was from Persia.

Garlung looked unfamiliar at first. He wore his hair much shorter than in the dream world, perhaps due to the nature of his work. He appeared older, more vulnerable here in the physical world. My attention focused on his arms and hands, which were scarred, calloused, and burned from the ovens and other kitchen duties. I felt the cold, eager stare of Kotan Runa, watching for any reaction as I made these observations. He knew my hands were not healed enough for this kind of work, yet I refused to flinch at the thought. I turned my glance to Garlung's face.

When our eyes met, he brightened, and I recognized the youthful being I had met that first day. No words were spoken, but his fresh, warm smile spoke of the friendship we shared.

A darkness broke our mood as Kotan Runa stepped forward, exerting his influence. "It looks as if you have found a place you prefer," he said, his narrowed eyes darting shiftily between us. "Good! Mukanume, you may show Lobnear-Wa his chores." With the air of a haughty ruler, he strode up the stairs, alone.

That night in the dream world, I walked with Garlung in the shimmering halls of the monastery.

"Why do you work in the kitchen?" I probed.

"So we can eat!" he answered with a youthful laugh.

"Why do you not work in the kitchen in the dream world?" I pressed, unsatisfied.

"The kitchen is where Kotan Runa placed me over one hundred years ago," he answered musingly.

"Where is Kotan Runa's place in the dream world?"

"He chooses not to have one," he replied simply.

"Why?" I asked, but Garlung only smiled. After a silence, he finally continued, "Kotan Runa is in charge of daily activities of the physical temple. I serve under him while in the physical, and I do so gladly. But in the dream world, I am one of the temple's guardians."

We continued in silence, but I understood that Kotan Runa did not wish to subject himself to Garlung. I thought it strange, for I sensed that Garlung never acted unjustly toward anyone.

Weeks passed without incident in the physical temple. The work in the kitchen was hot, exhausting, and at times dangerous, but fulfilling. Through the days, Garlung never mentioned our visits in the temple of the dream world. It was only as my body began to regain strength that I started to remember more and more events from the dream world.

In this same period, I found myself able to "read" from the Naacal Records and the Records of the Kros while performing some of the more repetitive kitchen chores. Days later, while I was inwardly perusing the records, Kotan Runa entered the kitchen with the look of a parent who is about to reprimand a child—and enjoy it.

"Your mind is not on your work, Lobnear-Wa," he said, a menacing tone in his voice. His clear, blue eyes turned a cold gray, and pugnacity dripped from the pores of his vibrant, white skin.

I remained quiet.

"Certain records within this temple are to be seen only with the abbot's permission, or with *my* permission, if it is in my jurisdiction. When you are working, you are to concentrate solely on your task at hand. There are many physical dangers in the kitchen, and you jeopardize your fellow workers. Since it is within my authority to guard the well-being of the temple in these matters, I will be watching you carefully. For the good of all, cease your inner wanderings!" he ordered forcefully.

His last words echoed off the white stone walls like the cracking of a whip as Sri Fubbi Quantz entered the kitchen. His steps made no sound, but the Master's presence was known by the sheer vibrancy of the air surrounding him.

Kotan Runa's mood changed immediately as he bowed in obeisance. Acknowledging us, Sri Fubbi Quantz said to me, "Your efforts in the temple are appreciated. If you wish, come tonight to the main hall in the dream world. After the lecture, we will visit the Kadath Inscriptions." Turning to Garlung, he asked, "Can this be arranged?"

Garlung nodded silently. Sri Fubbi Quantz smiled to the rest and left quietly. Kotan Runa shot me a malevolent gaze. Turning brusquely, he left the kitchen through an opposite stairway.

By day, the temple was bathed in gentle sunlight. Its corridors lay placid, with only the temple monks rippling the air as they quietly and efficiently performed their daily duties. But now, in the dream world, it was filled with hundreds of visitors escorted by those same monks.

Garlung led me to a small chamber where the Kadath Inscriptions were stored. There were no shelves or stones with writing on them, only a simple room with floor cushions and plain white walls. After showing me where to sit, Garlung bowed and left me alone in the small room. Closing my eyes, I contemplated on the Light and Sound.

Soon, a warm, familiar presence filled the room. I opened my eyes to find Sri Fubbi Quantz standing before me. As I moved to greet him, he smiled and motioned for me to remain seated and relaxed.

"Look before you!" he whispered. At first I saw nothing more than the blank walls, then they suddenly faded into darkness. Countless stars illumined a night sky.

I gazed into the deep space and soon realized the blue-and-white "stars" were not stars as I had originally believed, but beings—the Living ECK Masters of the ages. Focusing on one of them, I drew closer. His brilliance was so great, I feared such a great light would burn, but there was only a soothing warmth. I shielded my eyes from the light with my arm.

"Sri Yaubl Sacabi," Sri Fubbi Quantz explained. "This was my teacher. He will have much to teach you."

The being's image blended into the light, obscuring his features. A high, piercing sound echoed inside my head, and a voice beckoned me, "Come closer . . . closer."

Unable to resist its call, I moved toward the whiteness. The nearer I moved to this great light, the more I felt what I perceived as my self-identity dissipating, ceasing to exist.

"Do not fear," the voice encouraged, but I could go

no further. Lingering on the edge of the darkness and facing the absolute whiteness, I froze, afraid of losing myself. Clutching for my old identity, I tumbled backward into the darkness. The light shrank until it was only a small speck once more.

"There will be other times—we will meet again," the voice echoed as it faded.

A scrambling panic beat back my fear. I struggled to return to the light, begging for another chance, but my opportunity was gone. The darkness enveloped me in a soft, numbing haze. I drifted deeper into the unconscious abyss of sleep.

10
Reflections

The next morning, Kotan Runa marched into the kitchen, ignoring Garlung and Mukanume. He stopped where Zansar and I roasted grain. We lay the shallow pan on some bricks to cool while the open fire licked the air with yellow tongues.

"You are doing well in the kitchen. I thank you!" he commended huskily.

"It is you I wish to thank," I returned, remaining on guard.

"Tell me, are there more ECK Masters than there are stars?" he asked with a touch of sarcasm.

I knew he had been eavesdropping in my dream world the night before. My solar plexus burned, weakening my will. The angrier I became, the stronger he seemed to grow. He stood proud, hands on his hips. His lips turned up slightly, sneering as if daring me to fight. He held his head high so he could look down upon me, emphasizing his superior size.

No words were spoken, but inwardly, his thought impressions barraged me, "Weakling! You are food for the maggots! Come! Challenge me! Fight me! Let me drink your simpering life-force away!"

It felt like nails were being driven into my forehead. Kotan Runa surrounded my mind with his attacking judgments, tightening and squeezing out any thoughts of my own. Zansar held my shoulder as I reached for the corner of the table to steady myself.

"Perhaps you need more sleep!" Kotan Runa mocked as he eased his attack, satisfied at his exhibition of superiority. I could not see his face, but he stood gloating over me before strutting away.

Days passed without my physically confronting Kotan Runa, but inwardly, the vitality of my physical body was drained by the fight that raged within. Stinging bands of pain would periodically seize my head while I worked in the kitchen, and with each shock of agony came the recurring memory of Kotan Runa's taunts. Sleep was my only escape.

Later, I met Sri Fubbi Quantz in the dream world, alone in the hushed moments before dawn after the evening's classes had concluded. Without words, I followed him to the main hall.

All was dark in the cavernous hall except for a sheltered light at one end. In front of a small, partially hidden nave, we came upon a monk, so still I did not notice his presence until he bowed. As his eyes met Sri Fubbi Quantz's, the monk moved away silently. In this nave was the glowing light of a thousand candles—but there were no candles. There was only a large, open book on a stand. Light flowed from the book's pages.

"The Shariyat-Ki-Sugmad," the ECK Master spoke tenderly, as if in the presence of a newborn child. "You have been shown the Naacal Records and the Records of the Kros—both contain the annals of mankind. But of all in the universe, there is none as precious as the Shariyat-Ki-Sugmad, the 'Way of the Eternal.'

"As men, our words last only as long as others

remember them; the Word of God, the HU, lasts forever. Listen: When you hear your heart softly beating and your lifeblood flowing through your body, when you hear the wind passing through the mountains, listen carefully. You are hearing the sound of HU."

He continued in a hushed reverence, "The pages of this sacred book reflect the HU. Soul knows and lives by the true nature of the HU and, in doing so, recognizes Its own true nature. Come, Lobnear-Wa—read the holy book of ECK."

There was no writing on the pages, only the golden Light, radiant, more life-giving than the midday sun.

A great desire welled in my heart; a desire to love all life. An inherent understanding of all things was mine. Within the pages of this book rested all the secrets of the universe: all the joys humanity could desire and all the answers to any question one could ever ask. The ECK Master touched my shoulder lightly.

"The Shariyat-Ki-Sugmad is also a mirror. What lives in your heart is what you will read in its pages. If there are many opinions in the reader, the book will have less to say. Come."

I was troubled as we walked to the stairway that led back to my quarters, and I confided in him. "There has been little silence, little stillness in my heart since I have been in Katsupari.

"As a monk in the monastery at Thung-yule, I was trained in the art of freeing myself of all passions. Yet, since coming here I find there is one that stirs anger within me. Was my training false? Was all for naught?"

Sri Fubbi Quantz's eyes bore into mine with a fierce penetration, but his words were soft, "True strength can only occur when there is no longer fear in your heart, only love. Then the fears of others cannot be reflected. Look in your heart now. Who is it that brings you turmoil?"

Sadly, I reckoned that my own anger and fear was tied with Kotan Runa's image.

"Remember—the stronger image will have its way in your life. You must consciously choose anger and fear or compassion and love."

"Reading the Shariyat-Ki-Sugmad and meeting Sri Yaubl Sacabi in the Kadath Inscriptions mark a new beginning in your search. You now have the keys you have been looking for. You have already met the one who can teach you more, Sri Yaubl Sacabi. He can be found in the city of Agam Des."

His brow furrowed at these words, as if he were looking into the future. Breaking the silence of his deep thought, like a pebble dropped in a glass-smooth lake, he looked slowly to me.

"Lobnear-Wa, singing HU is the expression of SUGMAD's essence. Herein lies the sacredness of ITS name. If you cared deeply for another, would you utter the words *I love you* in a monotonous, chanting manner as is done in many of the gompas? No? Then so it is with singing HU. HU is a love song to the One who encompasses all that you love, have ever loved, or will ever love in life. HU is a love song to the Creator of love itself."

"Master, to love the Creator—to know God—that is what I live for!"

He nodded his head slowly, "In time your dream may come true, if in fact this is your greatest desire."

"It is my greatest desire! I have no other dream!" I added passionately, holding a fist to my chest.

The ECK Master's eyes turned upward, as if he were listening to instructions from a secret, yet all-pervasive voice. Without lowering his gaze to me, he spoke, "In three days, we will mark the solstice. All in the temple will meet in the great hall for the Council. Perhaps it will aid your quest."

11
The Council

While evenings in the dream world were spent in study of the Shariyat-Ki-Sugmad with Sri Fubbi Quantz, days in the kitchen were filled with tension. Kotan Runa missed no opportunity to exert his authority over me.

The morning after Sri Fubbi Quantz mentioned the Council meeting, however, Kotan Runa displayed a change in his attitude. Pulling me to one side in the kitchen, he spoke in hushed tones.

"Your duties are going well, I trust?" he asked cordially. It was the first time since my arrival at Katsupari that he expressed heartfelt consideration. The usual underlying threat was absent. I nodded curtly, still wary of his true intentions.

"Lobnear-Wa, I have been strict with you for a purpose. Though it may seem my treatment of you has been harsh, it has not been without reason. You see, I am one of the guardians of the temple. All who visit Katsupari can do so only with my permission, unless otherwise stated by Fubbi Quantz. If I did not use discretion in choosing who enters the temple, it would soon lose its integrity, harmony, and strength, and could no longer function in the capacity it must."

I searched his eyes for deceit but found none. His words seemed sincere—but was it the truth? He continued, "There are those who are ambitious and perhaps envious of my position, but I will tell you this: I do not find joy in many of my duties. I do not enjoy disciplining others. I do it only to serve the ECK, and I will do my best, even if it means severing that which is dear to me!

"I tell you this not to sway your opinion, for I care not what others think of me. I tell you this for the good of the whole, and for your own knowledge. Perhaps in time you will understand."

He smiled benevolently and began to leave, but stopped after a few steps and turned.

"There is one truth I would share with you. It has been my experience that it never benefits one to issue complaints against others in the temple; rather, it only points out the defects in the one making the complaints. It is often a ploy of the weak. I have seen it make bitter men out of complainers."

With this thought, he left me. Why did he change his attitude toward me just before the Council? Did he fear my close association with Sri Fubbi Quantz? Or that I would reveal his true nature to all in the monastery? I sensed much depended on the outcome of the Council.

At midnight, we met in the great hall. Fifty maroon-robed monks took seats on floor cushions. Garlung and Kotan Runa were there, as well as Mukanume and Zansar and many others I had come to know during my stay. Sri Fubbi Quantz entered near the front of the assembly through a small, partially hidden doorway. All in the hall began to sing HU, the ancient name of the Creator, the SUGMAD. As it permeated the hall like a tide rolling into a shallow bay, I felt its strengthening, nurturing sound. Gradually, the singing ebbed into silence, and a contemplative period followed.

"May the blessings be," Sri Fubbi Quantz said softly, ending the contemplation. He motioned to Kotan Runa. "You may begin the Council."

Kotan Runa stood slowly from his cushion and surveyed all in the hall.

"Are there words to be shared?" he asked. No one spoke.

"Then I, Kotan Runa, have words." With each deep, heaving breath, the light seemed to leave his face. Transfixed, I stared aghast as his features contorted into the darkening image of the naljorpa. His golden-white hair turned a greasy, matted black, and lice danced off his blackened face. His shriveled lips curled up, revealing broken, yellowed teeth. He looked menacingly about, riveted an evil stare at me, turned away, and drew another deep breath. By the time he exhaled, the darkness receded, leaving him looking like himself again. Had I been the only one to witness this terrible transformation? He spoke in a deep voice, choosing his words with care.

"There has been a breach of harmony within the walls of the temple." A hot pulse of alarm shot through the crowd in the hall.

"It is the custom of the temple that if one of the monks objects to an outsider's presence, the outsider must be expelled. I hereby exercise this right, and request that Lobnear-Wa take his leave of the temple at dawn. I say this with no malice in my heart, but only for the good of the temple's welfare and the promotion of harmony. If there is another who would speak for the outsider, let him speak now, or the final decision will pass to the abbot of the temple, Fubbi Quantz."

His words struck me hard. Expelled from the temple! How could this be? The shock of it held me in a disbelieving stupor. Only when Garlung, Mukanume, and Zansar stood up slowly from their seats in the hall did I realize the severity of events.

"I speak for the outsider," Garlung said softly.

"As do we," echoed Mukanume and Zansar.

"You present no justifiable cause for me to change my decision," Kotan Runa replied tersely.

He turned to Sri Fubbi Quantz. "I leave the final decision to the abbot. It is the custom of the temple — for an outsider to remain within the temple, *all* monks must desire him to stay. If there is but one voice against, he must take his leave. I stand firm in my voice against!" Kotan Runa sat down in his place sternly, arms folded solidly across his chest.

All eyes turned to Sri Fubbi Quantz, who remained calm throughout the turbulent sequence of events. Rising slowly, he addressed me quietly.

"Lobnear-Wa, it is your right to speak on your own behalf. Is there reason in your own eyes that may justify your staying at the temple?"

As I stood to speak, my mind reeled, and Kotan Runa's words returned to me. "Those who complain only reveal their own weaknesses." His seed was well-planted. I wanted to defend myself, to right the many wrongs I felt he had committed against me. But I considered the consequences of voicing a complaint against him. Was it cowardice or temperance that made me hesitate? The inner struggle split my will, and I looked helplessly to Sri Fubbi Quantz. "I have nothing to say on my behalf."

Sri Fubbi Quantz turned to the assembly of monks.

"It is as Kotan Runa states. As long as there is one at the temple that wishes an outsider to leave, it must be so. This is my decision."

My hands and feet tingled, then I lost all feeling in them. I gasped for air. I could not believe what I had heard! Sri Fubbi Quantz continued, his calm, hooded eyes surveying the chelas.

"Is there anyone in the Council who would have words? If not, I call this Council closed." As he rose, all the other monks in the hall stood and quietly filed out. Before he left, Garlung cast me a look of great sorrow and loss. I stood transfixed, my stomach painfully empty, and my feet leaden. I did not understand what was happening. Dazed, I turned to walk out of the hall, automatically following. But my attention was drawn to the front. There stood Sri Fubbi Quantz, directing a penetrating gaze at me.

Our eyes locked, and for that brief instant, there was the knowingness that I had not been deserted. Slowly, he turned and left through the small front entrance. As I stood alone, the Light and Sound of the ECK enveloped me in a brilliant whiteness. Somehow I felt that my life had ended and begun in the same moment.

12
Banished

The view of the mountains through my windows shone gold and pink against the fading, deep-blue night, mercifully chasing away my twisted memories of the Council. Like a condemned man awaiting execution at dawn, I savored each breath I took while still in the temple.

With the sun rising through the lowest valleys of the mountains, Kotan Runa appeared at my door with three monks dressed in thick, hooded chubas and boots, laden with ropes and provisions for my journey. Kotan Runa looked at me long and expressionlessly before speaking.

"The daylight must be used wisely if you are to make your way through the mountain passes." There was no malice or gloating in his eyes or voice, only compassion. He knew the trials of the cold that lay ahead.

"I have provided enough for you to make safe ground—ropes, your chuba, boots, food, and three guides. They will escort you to the pass, where you can make your way to Shire Nor, a two weeks' trek. To attempt to follow them back to the temple would be futile; remember, you were allowed to find the temple the first time. You will not be so fortunate if you attempt to seek it again." I nodded in acknowledgment.

Putting on my thick chuba and boots was the first stage of separation from the temple. As we tramped to the main floor in our bulky garb, I felt alienated from the refined monks. Icy winds and snow tore through the sparse hall like hungry invaders as one of the tall, wooden doors was swung wide with great effort by the three monks. Deep snow covered the ground as we trudged past the spot where I was first found so many months before.

The monks unfurled the ropes amid a biting wind, then we rappeled down the face of the sheer cliffs. Swirling masses of blinding snow and punishing cold quickly obliterated thoughts of Katsupari.

At the end of three days' climb down the mountain, we reached the bottom. Falling snow blocked our sight, and we remained linked together by ropes so we would not become separated. In the evening, we camped in a small clearing. I drifted off to a memoryless sleep.

When I awoke, I found snow laid over me like a thick, powdery blanket. My companions had left in the night, long before the snow had accumulated. Tracing their departure would be impossible.

They had left me ample supplies: ropes, enough barley and yak butter for two weeks, and the blanket that covered me. The way to Shire Nor was apparent: there was only one path out of that small clearing at the foot of the steep mountains.

Dusting the snow off myself and the supplies, I trekked southward through a narrow pass. But after that, there was no clear trail to follow in the mountains. I was on my own.

* * *

I counted eight days since I had left the temple, when a storm finally made travel impossible. A narrow fissure in the rock face provided temporary shelter from the punishing wind and snow.

A drift piled high, sealing me away from the blizzard. I eagerly grasped the first opportunity in days for undisturbed rest. Closing my eyes, I concentrated on warmth through tumo. But instead of the dark blankness of sleep which I had hoped to achieve, a vision of Sri Fubbi Quantz appeared.

"Why did you allow me to be cast from the temple?" I asked, with hurt surprise.

"The will of the ECK will be," he answered softly, his words drifting in and out with the muffled howl of the wind.

"Was it truly the will of the ECK, or was it the will of Kotan Runa?" I asked aggressively.

"Kotan Runa fills a position in the temple," the phantomlike voice whispered.

"You condone his actions and behavior?" I pressed, confused.

"I condone Spirit. That is all. In the worlds of matter, the laws of matter are followed. The hungry wolf slaughters the meekest lamb to weed out weakness in the flock," the image replied.

"Is that all I was? A weak, helpless lamb? Would it have been better to have fought and brought disharmony into the temple? I could show them how strong I am! I'll fight all life. I shall take it by the scruff and wring it into submission! I shall return to Katsupari!" I shouted, with clenched fists.

"What is it about Kotan Runa that you hate so much?" he questioned, cutting through my outburst with a knife of quiet truth.

"I . . . I do not hate. It is the naljorpa inside him that I wish to destroy once and for all."

"And is this naljorpa truly within Kotan Runa, or is it within yourself?" he replied.

My memory raced back to the filthy naljorpa who had thrown rotting food into my face outside Shire Nor. I remembered the repulsion I had experienced as he inhaled the worms and laughed. Did he exist now as a parasite in my own body?

"But what of the naljorpa I saw in Kotan Runa's face? Did he not have this same parasite within himself? Because I was able to see it, does that mean it must exist only in myself?"

"It is true we sometimes see in others what exists only within ourselves," the voice said, fading until it was difficult to hear.

"You are an enlightened being. How can you not see this facet of him? Or do you see only sweet innocence and love in his eyes?" I questioned bitterly.

The inner vision returned stronger for an instant, "I do not judge sweet innocence or evil parasites. I do not attempt to shield my eyes from reality. Nor do I attempt to change the wolf into the lamb or the lamb into the wolf."

"Then by what authority do you maintain abbotship of the monastery?" I challenged, trying to understand.

"I allow neither good nor evil to sway my viewpoint. With no personal desires to narrow my sight, I see life through the eyes of Spirit, with no judgments or mental comparisons. The ECK is like the sky that surrounds the earth. It sees all and permeates all but does not judge life on the planet. Yet without It, there could be no life."

A realization that I could have been mistaken about the occurrences in the temple, and misled in my ideas about God, crept over me like a cold, deathlike hand.

"Then I have been a fool—a weakling fool!" I said in bitter anguish.

The voice of the vision dissipated and became the hissing of the inner sounds. Outside the wall of snow, silence pervaded. I dug myself out to see the sun shining through still, cloudless skies.

Sweeping away the snow, I pulled out my remaining supplies. I worked my way to a high point of rocks to see where I was. From the summit, I saw the mouth of a large valley, and beyond, smaller, rolling hills. Wisps of gray smoke rose from the horizon. It would be the village of Shire Nor.

13
Lo-tsa-ba and Shen

Two days later, I reached the source of the smoke. The smoke undulated black and fleeting from the chimney of a small, isolated sod hut on the side of a snow-covered hill. Far from the rest of the village, the hut squatted in a shallow valley. As I drew near, a small mongrel protected the property by yapping a high, piercing warning to its owner.

The door was nothing more than a few splintered boards tied together with fraying rope strands. It scraped open, and a small man with thin, straggly hair and sooty face cautiously poked his head out, squinting in my direction. In a high, frightened voice, he quickly shouted, "Who are you? Are you a devil? Are you a tax collector for the prince? A bandit? I have nothing! Go away!"

"I am none of those. My name is Lobnear-Wa. I have traveled many days from the north. I need food and shelter, and have gold coins to pay."

At the mention of gold, the man opened his door slightly wider and called his dog away from me.

"Where did you say you come from?" he asked, more politely, but still cautiously.

"From the mountains to the north. I have been in a monastery for most of the winter."

The man narrowed his eyes accusingly, "There is still much snow in the passes. There are no monasteries nearby that I know of. How did you survive? You must be a devil!"

"No, it is true. I have been traveling almost twelve days since I was cast out of a hidden temple. I finally sought shelter among some rocks. Snow sealed me in until the storm ceased. I was born in Thung-yule. Look! I still have a few barley grains in my bag. A devil would have no need for food. I am man!" I countered, showing the few grains I had in the bottom of my sack.

"How did you survive the cold all those days?" he hissed.

"I was once a monk. I trained in the art of tumo. I know how to raise my body heat," I explained.

The little man stroked the stubble on his chin and muttered to himself, "Tumo... hmmm... tumo... hmmm." Then looking up at me sharply, he demanded, "Let me see those coins!"

Moving slowly so I would not frighten him, I produced the two small coins and held them out to him.

"Lay them on the ground and back away," he said nervously.

I did as he requested. He emerged from the hut, bent down gingerly, watching my every move while he quickly darted glances to the gold. His hand snatched up the coins like a whiplash. Holding them close to his eyes, he examined them minutely, while watching me at the same time. He turned them over several times and bit one of them hard with his back teeth.

"These coins are very old! Where did you get them?" he demanded.

"They were given to me by the head lama in the monastery at Thung-yule."

Cocking his head to one side, his eyes narrowed again, and he laid the coins carefully back on the snow. "I won't take them. There is magic in them. You are the only one who can use them. Take them back!"

"I am still in need of food and shelter," I reminded him.

"Wait here!" he ordered, backing into his hut. Moments later, he came out with a long pointed pole and a small knife. Tossing the knife at my feet, he held the pole pointed at me like a spear.

"Cut yourself! If you are a devil, your blood will be black. Cut yourself and prove you are man," he said tersely, jabbing the stick at the air in front of me.

Slowly, I picked up the small knife and, on the upper part of my wrist, made a small slice. Red blood oozed from the thin line and dripped on the snow. The dog inched forward, led by his sniffing nose to lick the blood from the snow as I dropped the knife to the ground. Picking it up, the man breathed a sigh of relief and lowered his stick.

"I am Lo-tsa-ba. Come in. Come in."

I followed as he shuffled into the smoky, darkened hut. Inside, a small fire glowed warmly. As my eyes adjusted, I saw a low, wooden table near the hearth and another room beyond. Slightly alarmed, I sensed the presence of another with us. Huddled near the fire, a small, crouching figure peered at me with shining eyes.

"My daughter, Shen," Lo-tsa-ba said, nodding to the diminutive woman. "Shen, some tsampa and some chiang to drink."

My eyes had become accustomed to the dim light of the hut, but I was still unable to make out Shen's features. She appeared slightly younger than I. Tiny and delicate, her hair was pulled back on her head. She moved with quick, graceful movements, taking small steps as she gathered some wooden bowls and cups.

"I have my own bowl," I said, pulling it from my sack and handing it to her. As she timidly took the bowl from my hand, I saw her face more clearly.

Her eyes were like a small animal's eyes: trusting, yet alert. Her face was wide and smooth, with a wide mouth and thin lips. High cheekbones tapered to a slender chin.

Lo-tsa-ba motioned jerkily for me to sit on a furry black skin on the ground while the milky porridge and foaming chiang was served. Shen did not sit with us but attended the black pots hanging over the fire.

Lo-tsa-ba drank the steaming chiang from a strange white cup. Noticing my curious stare, he gulped from the cup, and waved it at me. "The skull of my wife. She died many cycles ago. I made a drinking cup of it, so I may remember her fondly. She no longer has use of it, so now it comforts me when I drink." Gently cradling the little white cup, he pointed across the room. "I keep the rest of her bones hanging above the fireplace," he said, nodding to a yak-skin sack on the wall.

"My daughter was married to a farmer. He fell behind in his crop payments to the prince, who is controlled by the Black Hat Karma-pa lamas. The taxes were too great. When he could not pay his share, he was taken to prison, where he died. Shen is childless, and no other man wanted a barren woman. So she has come to live with me."

The course of the sorry tale dampened his mood. "Now I am at risk of losing my land as well. The sun and spring air do not warm my fields soon enough to plant and yield enough barley. No other farmer plants as close to the ice and snow of the mountains as I. And for good reason; this ground is the last to thaw. But it is all I have. I will not take your magic gold coins, but if you wish to stay, you may help me plant when the ground has thawed."

The hot chiang and tsampa was the first warm meal I had had since leaving Katsupari. It was comforting, but I had no intention of staying long in any place until I found Sri Yaubl Sacabi, whom Fubbi Quantz had told me was at Agam Des. I was ready to say no and take my leave when Shen came to the table to refill our cups and bowls. She spoke no words, nor did she look at me, but the air about her vibrated strongly. I had never before felt such an energy, and though my mind wanted to thank Lo-tsa-ba and leave quickly, I found my mouth saying otherwise.

"Yes, yes, I will stay, but I know nothing about farming. I was raised to be a lama." The words were spoken like the sealing of a contract. My mind flurried and questioned my sanity, while my eyes watched Lo-tsa-ba—but my full attention followed Shen's every move.

"Good! You may sleep in the other room. Shen and I will sleep here. Until the thaw begins, there are preparations to be made for planting. Rest today. Tomorrow we will begin work," he said heartily, taking a large swallow of chiang and smacking his lips.

I did not look at Shen while she stirred the contents of one of the black pots, but I could feel her eyes watching me.

14
The Eyes of a Small Animal

Weeks passed, and the ground was eventually soft enough to break. Lo-tsa-ba and I took turns at the ox-drawn plow, while Shen planted the seeds. In all this time, her eyes had never met mine. She never spoke to me nor called my name. Any instructions were given to me by Lo-tsa-ba. On occasion, Shen spoke to her father, but rarely when I was present. Each day, she quietly prepared hot meals for us, not avoiding me, but never lowering the invisible barrier either.

It was not long before I looked forward to watching her every move. Was it my imagination, or was she growing more beautiful by the day? When she served our meals, her sleeve would sometimes brush my shoulder or arm, sending hot-and-cold shivers through my body. Outwardly, I tried to remain calm, but inwardly, I was both terrified and excited. Every pore in my body became enlivened, like flowers open to drink the sun's nurturing rays. Many times I desired to speak to her, but there never seemed to be a reason for words. I was content to enjoy her presence, and she seemed content to do the same.

As I watched Shen, Lo-tsa-ba watched me and stifled a smile, pretending not to notice how my attention was drawn to his daughter.

At night, before sleeping, I dreamed of her. I wondered what it would be like to touch her hands, to hold her. I imagined her eyes. Though my mind did not understand, my heart knew the message they communicated.

One morning, when the seeding of the land was nearly completed, three horsemen appeared at the top of a hill. With the sun behind them, they were covered in shadows: an ominous omen.

"Gar-pas—guards of the Black Hats," Lo-tsa-ba hissed as he shielded his eyes from the sun. "They come to remind me of my debts," he said as he angrily urged the ox onward.

In a burst, the Gar-pas charged down the hill, heedless of the damage their horses did in stirring up the freshly plowed and seeded land. Heavily armed with spears and swords and covered in armor, they seemed too ready for bloodshed. Yak-hair tassles flowed from pointed spikes on their helmets, mixing with their own long hair and enhancing their fierce, animal-like appearance. The large horses snorted and stamped anxiously, barely contained by their riders. The guard in the center, the largest, seemed to be the leader. He rode to within an arm's length of Lo-tsa-ba. Head held high, he haughtily looked down at us.

"Lo-tsa-ba! We come to pay you a courtesy visit from the prince and the lamasery!" he sneered.

"I need no reminder of your taxes!" Lo-tsa-ba growled, baring his teeth.

"No, I suppose you have a good memory, don't you?" the soldier returned. The other two laughed at his comments.

"But then you don't need to remember anything but the day we come for our share of the crops! We shall not forget you owe us many sacks of grain from the last cycle!" Laughing, he turned his horse, raining clods of earth on us as he and the others galloped away.

Lo-tsa-ba stood motionless, except for his lower jaw which shook with rage. Tears welled up in the corners of his eyes, scooted down his cheeks, and salted the earth.

"The Gar-pas, the tax collectors, the prince, and the Black Hats that control them all—they laugh and scorn me for being poor. Though I have little, it is *they* who are poor for they are never satisfied with what they have. No matter how much wealth they hoard, it will never be enough!"

The remainder of the day's labor seemed tainted, as if the seeds we planted would somehow grow deformed or be stunted. At dark, Shen prepared our dinner. No one had spoken since the three horsemen had left. Shen carried the black pot of tsampa to the table. As she poured the hot porridge into my bowl, her hand slipped. The steaming mush poured into my lap. I jumped up quickly, causing her to drop the pot on the ground. I was not hurt, but for an instant all three of us froze. Suddenly, she put her hands to her face, and like a cloud overladen with rain, she burst into tears and ran out of the hut.

Lo-tsa-ba sat bewildered with his mouth opened, as I shook off the rest of the steaming white gruel.

"I will find Shen," I said to Lo-tsa-ba as I ran after her.

Finding her was not difficult. Her sobs led me to the rear of the hut, where she huddled with her hands covering her face. I did not know why I came after her, nor did I know what to say, except that I knew somehow I had to express my feelings for her.

"I will help you pay the debt—I will help," I offered clumsily, not knowing what else to say to make things better. She stopped crying. Suddenly, she ran back into the house. It was dark outside, but I thought I saw her fighting back a smile as she left me. I did not understand.

The next day while in the fields, I turned to Lo-tsa-ba. "I have no riches, no yaks, no horses, nothing of my own that you can use, except my toil on your land. I have nothing to offer you but this. If I work until your farm is out of debt from the Black Hats, will you give me permission to marry your daughter?"

Lo-tsa-ba dropped the reins of the ox and drew his head back in surprise. He looked away at the ground, then back to me, smiling and nodding.

"Yes, yes! You have my permission! You may have my daughter. Yes!" He laughed aloud.

"Come! Come into the house! I will tell Shen. She will be happy. We will eat now and be happy!" Walking back to the hut, he put his arm around my shoulder. Lo-tsa-ba burst through the shabby door, arms stretched out to his daughter. "Shen! Lobnear-Wa wishes you to be his wife! As of this moment, you two are married!"

Unperturbed by Lo-tsa-ba's gregariousness, Shen rose graciously from the ground where she tended the fire and slowly lifted her head. The eyes of a small animal met mine for the first time. On her face was a smile, radiating the light of an inner world I had longed to know.

* * *

During the harvest, the moods of Lo-tsa-ba and Shen became increasingly tense. The sacking of the grain was done in total silence. When the work was done and the sacks counted, Lo-tsa-ba sat disheartened. There were not enough to satisfy the taxes demanded by the Black Hats.

For four days, we waited in dread for the Gar-pas to arrive and take away the rewards of our labors. On the morning of the fifth day, several yaks and their drivers and seven armed Gar-pas appeared at the top of the hill, a slow-moving serpent from which there was no escape. They arrived on our land with arrogance, as if it belonged to them and we were little more than animals to be tended.

While the yak drivers counted and loaded our grain sacks, two Gar-pas searched the hut for any grain we may have hidden for ourselves. Others searched the surrounding land.

"You will not find any hidden grain. This is all we have!" Lo-tsa-ba cried bitterly.

The chief collector, clad in rich, red silk garments, strolled indolently around us. "I will have my men look just the same. You have so little, it would seem to me that you must be hiding some. Of course, you know the penalty for withholding taxes is death."

The head driver brought a tally of the sacks, and the chief collector checked the figures with his records. The guards returned from their search empty-handed.

"You are again several sacks short this year. If you do not pay the full amount owed in the next cycle, your land will be forfeited to the prince. You will fall at his feet for mercy. As it is, we are more than generous in leaving you one sack to live on until next harvest," the collector stated without emotion.

"The amount you ask is too much; the land will not yield more! Surely you can see this! This land is too close to the ice and mountains. It will never produce as many sacks of barley as other farms.

"And only one sack of grain? There are three of us!

One sack barely fed two last year!" Lo-tsa-ba pleaded excitedly.

The collector merely raised one eyebrow and turned his back to us. Barking orders to the drivers, they drove to the next hapless farm.

15
The Harvest

We decided the only way to meet the greedy demands of the tax collector was to clear more land on the hillside nearer the ice. Smaller boulders were pried loose with wooden levers and rolled away. The rocky ground was cleared as much as possible before the snows fell; this was all we could do until spring. It was a slim chance but our only hope to grow the needed grain.

The cooler weather of late autumn moved us to spend more of our days in the confines of the hut, allowing my attention to turn more to Shen.

"Lobnear-Wa," she whispered in a quiet moment one night, as the last of the evening's fire died down. "Why did you choose me?"

I looked into her wide, deep eyes and held her small face in my hands while we lay close to each other. I did not know why—my heart compelled me to be with her. Beyond doubt, beyond all reason and fear, my desire for her overshadowed all else. Many times I was amazed and helpless that my feelings for her would hold such sway with me, but it was a desire I never regretted and never fought.

"Because. Because in you, I see the beauty of God. I was told that God is love, but those words never helped me understand God. When I am with you, I somehow know and understand." I looked into her shining eyes and knew she did not comprehend.

"Because when you are close to me, you bring me such joy that I want to give you all I am," I said. She understood this, and her eyes brightened as she held me closer.

When the spring thaw began to melt the ice and snow from the mountains and hillsides, we prepared to sow the ground. The last to be seeded was the rocky hillside we had cleared before winter. As we struggled with the plow one afternoon, three familiar, ominous figures on horseback appeared on the distant hilltop.

They descended on us like predators. Lo-tsa-ba cringed behind the plow, cursing them. I moved Shen away from their path and ran to restrain the ox, who was frightened by the charging horses.

The leader of the Gar-pas laughed at Lo-tsa-ba, "Coward! Do you think this meager patch of rock will yield the needed taxes? You are fit to be nothing better than a slave—which is what you will be when you cannot pay your share of taxes to the prince and the monastery! Enjoy your so-called freedom in the warm months, for when harvesttime comes, you will spend the rest of your life in chains!" They rode off to threaten another poor farmer in a similar predicament.

The Gar-pas' taunts spurred the three of us to greater determination. The rocky, barren ground gave us something to vent our rage upon, and the hard clods of earth broke under our persistence. Water from the stream could not be diverted to irrigate the sloping hillside; these crops had to be watered by hand. Each day we worked far past sunset to nurture our last hope.

When the autumn harvest was finished, we poured our precious grain into sacks. Our hopes rose with each one we filled. When the last sack was tied and counted, we hugged and rejoiced. There would be enough to pay the taxes, as well as enough to live on until the next spring.

That night, we sang and celebrated. But deep in my heart was a troubling issue I had long put off—the continuation of my search for Sri Yaubl Sacabi. The thought of betraying and leaving Lo-tsa-ba tore at me, but I had a plan.

"Lobnear-Wa! Why are you so sad all of a sudden? This is a time for rejoicing!" Lo-tsa-ba said, clapping his hand on my shoulder.

"Do you remember our original agreement?" I asked.

"What! You mean about working until I am out of debt so you could marry Shen? Do not be foolish! You are my son! If you think you are not welcome in my house any longer just because your debt is paid, you are wrong! You and Shen shall stay with me forever! This is your land and your house as well!" he said exuberantly, trying to bury any doubts with gusto.

"Listen to me, Lo-tsa-ba. I have thought on this for many days. My call is to find a teacher—one that I *must* find." I turned to Shen. "No matter what happens, I want you to know that I love you more than any in the world, yet I cannot ask you to leave your father if you do not wish to. You are free to stay on the land, or you may come with me." She started to answer, but I held a finger up, stopping her. "Wait. Hear me out."

To Lo-tsa-ba, I said, "With the grain that I would have eaten this winter, you can hire another man from

Shire Nor to help you with the fields. I will assist you in finding such a man. But there is another choice; the land can be sold, and all three of us can travel to find this teacher. We can all learn from him. We will be free of the tyrants who make us toil so hard to pay their taxes."

Lo-tsa-ba sat crumpled in a heap on the floor, a dazed look on his face.

"I have never done anything but farm. I was born on this land. My father was born on this land. Shen, you were born on this land. Could you bear to leave it? Tell me what to do!" he pleaded.

"Father, this is my home, but I could not bear to live without Lobnear-Wa—nor could I bear to live without you. I choose to go with my husband. Please come with us!"

Lo-tsa-ba looked far into space. "Nor could I bear to live without the two of you. But what would we do? How would we live?"

"We can find work as we travel. There are many ways," I remarked hopefully.

"Father, after we pay the taxes, we can offer our land for sale to one of the other farmers—or perhaps the prince will give us a fair price," Shen added.

Lo-tsa-ba nodded his head, "Yes, yes, perhaps we can sell the land. It would be good never to see those Gar-pas again!" A toothy grin spread slowly over his face.

16
The Tax Collector

The next morning, the predictable tax-collecting serpent appeared on the hilltop. We were glad to see them.

We stood confident as the collector's men counted the sacks of barley and the Gar-pas searched the rest of the land and the hut. When the final tally was brought to the tax collector, his eyebrows raised slightly.

"I see you have many more sacks than last year!"

"We farmed the side of the hill," Lo-tsa-ba pointed proudly, his hand extending toward the newly reaped land.

The collector nodded approvingly and turned with a sly grin. "Very good! But I am afraid it is not good enough."

"What do you mean?" Lo-tsa-ba's voice shook with panicked uncertainty.

"The administrating lama in Shire Nor has decided to raise your taxes. You still do not have enough grain. You will have to go to prison or become a slave of the prince. After all, he owes favors to larger farmers who could use this miserable patch."

Lo-tsa-ba's mouth worked excitedly, but nothing

came out. I moved closer to restrain him if he lost control of himself.

"There is perhaps one solution to your dilemma. Give us your daughter as a token of your good intention to pay off the taxes. The administrating lama is searching for pretty young women in debt these days," the collector proposed.

"No!" I shouted, lunging at the collector, but I did not get far. Expecting such a reaction, one of the horsemen knocked me to the ground with the blunt end of his spear. Two other guards quickly held me down at sword point and bound me with ropes.

"So we have a hero, eh?" the collector said, bemused. "Bind the old man as well. I have decided not to offer generous bargains to peasants."

As one of the guards moved to tie him up, Lo-tsa-ba reached for the collector's neck and began strangling him.

"Kill him!" the collector shouted to the guards. A guard drew his sword and slashed Lo-tsa-ba from behind, dropping him to the ground, dead. Shen screamed and pulled a small knife from the folds of her clothing. She rushed at the collector and stabbed him in the back. One of the horsemen rode up and ran his spear through her. Her eyes opened wide, a look of surprise on her face, and she fell facedown. Deep red blood oozed and soaked Shen's clothing. One of her arms, not quite dead yet, made a feeble effort to raise itself but flopped over limply.

I screamed in anguish as the last bit of life left her body. My mind, my sense of who I was — all was blinded by a terrible madness.

In panic and horror, I sobbed, begging them to kill me. Death was the only thing that could satisfy my rage if I could not wreak absolute destruction upon these murderers.

"No! You dogs! Kill me, too!" The words finally spilled in convulsive agony.

The guard poised his spear at my back as I lay on the ground, but the head guard shouted, "No! It is up to the administrating lama. Let him have the pleasure of condemning and watching this one die!"

They tied the bodies of Shen and Lo-tsa-ba to one of the horses and let them drag behind. I was tied to one of the other horses and forced to walk into the village, while the body of the tax collector was loaded on the wagon with the grain. My will was momentarily shattered. I felt like a wet rag, my fury was spent. I was now whimpering in a delirious hell. I could not resist. The only coherent thoughts I had were those of looking forward to arriving at the monastery in Shire Nor so I could meet my end of this life.

It took a full day to reach the village. Once in the monastery, I was thrown into a pit. For the first two days, I shivered like a rabid dog in the cold mud, no longer comprehending life. On the third day, I stopped shaking; the numbing madness seeming to recede. I was brought out to face my sentence. The administrating lama would be doing me a favor by executing me.

I was escorted by the guards to the chamber of justice where I would be sentenced. I saw the one who would pass judgment on me as he talked with his entourage at the front of the room. The right side of his face was crushed and horribly scarred. My body turned cold. The administrating lama was Tangri.

17
Judged

"So this is the peasant responsible for the death of my tax collector?" Tangri wheezed, in a raspy voice.

I said nothing and stared at the ground as was the custom of a peasant.

"Look up, peasant!" he demanded.

Slowly, I raised my head but dared not look at his face, for such an affront would have meant the gouging out of an eye. He cocked his head and narrowed his gaze.

"I believe I know you," he half-whispered. His eyes widened with recognition. "I shall never cease to believe in miracles! The gods have brought me Lobnear-Wa!" A grin of malevolent joy spread across his face, which he quickly stifled in the presence of his guards and scribes. His excitement caused him a coughing fit, and he clutched his heart, slumping deeper into his chair. The fall he had suffered in Thung-yule years ago had apparently taken a toll on his internal organs. After struggling for breath, he righted himself and assumed the detached air of a judge.

"The penalty for killing an official is death."

Turning to his guards, he ordered, "Tie him in the village square and whip him — but do not kill him yet."

* * *

Icy water splashed on my face, waking me from the unconsciousness of the flogging. The muddy water dripped off my body. My arms were still tied as I hung on a stake in the village square for all to see and mock. Tangri approached me. His men waited a dozen paces behind.

His voice seemed far away. I strained to hear him. My head throbbed with a dull pain. "You know you must die for your crimes, don't you?" he said calmly, quietly, almost with compassion. It was the gentlest voice I had ever heard from him.

"A crime such as yours usually requires a long, slow death. It could last many days. You would be a humiliated wretch begging for death. I could be merciful to you. I could grant you a swift and painless death."

I struggled to lift my head to face him as he pondered his next thoughts. I could only manage two uneven jerks before my neck went slack.

"There is only one condition — you must ask forgiveness for pushing me off the gompa stairs in Thungyule and mutilating my body. Ask, and I will grant forgiveness."

Struggling for clarity through my frayed senses, I tried to form my words. "Tangri, I did not push you from those stairs. It was the dobdob who caused your fall," I finally gasped.

"But you are responsible! Admit it!" he snarled sharply, dropping his facade of patience.

"I cannot ask forgiveness for what I did not do." The effort of speaking was too much. I gagged, spitting up blood.

Glaring at me, his voice became stiff, severe and self-righteous. "Very well. You arrived just in time for a journey, Lobnear-Wa. I have been invited to preside at the court of law in Drepung, the greatest monastery in Tibet, near Lhasa. This proves you were the fool and I was right. By being diplomatic, I moved from the small gompa at Thung-yule to administrating lama here in Shire Nor. Word travels quickly in political circles.

"The Yellow Hats are consolidating their power at Drepung. They have been watching my administrative abilities for collecting taxes and filling the monastery coffers in Shire Nor. Now, they have invited me to represent the Black Hats. They know I support good government, regardless of which hat they wear. I have prospered on what you originally turned down in Thung-yule," he taunted in a whisper. "I will make sure you stay alive, miserably alive."

To his guards, he barked tersely, "Untie him and shackle his hands and feet. We shall let him wear the wooden collar. And bring me the heads!" He held up to my face the heads of Lo-tsa-ba and my beloved wife, Shen.

"You shall drag these heads with you all the way to Drepung. You are much too proud, Lobnear-Wa. I shall help you overcome your pride and anger by breaking your stubborn will. Perhaps then you will come to your senses and ask for forgiveness."

The heads were strung on the chains that shackled my legs so that I would drag them behind me with each step I took. It would be a long trek to Lhasa.

The journey, which lasted nearly thirty days, had a different effect on me than I had originally thought. Instead of giving up to fatigue early on in the trek, my will to live grew fiercer with each torturous step, as the shackles dug into my ankles.

Eventually Tangri's train of twenty soldiers, supply carriers, attendants, and I reached the streets of Lhasa. I had never seen a city as large as this. I only wished it had been under more favorable circumstances.

Merchants hawked their wares in front of their shops, and hundreds of shoppers filled the streets. Stray dogs, oxen, yaks, goats, and sheep were everywhere. Lining the walkways were scores of beggars. Most were horribly disfigured: missing hands, limbs, eyes, or ears—the result of the cruel penal system of Lhasa. We stopped for supplies and rest in the marketplace before making the final short trip to Drepung monastery. I was forced to stand in the street, guarded by three of Tangri's men.

Suddenly, a commotion erupted in a nearby street. The crowd scattered in panic as a pack of six large brown dogs, which were chained together, began snapping in a mad frenzy. A mass of fangs and fur, they rushed in my direction. The chains and heavy wooden collar weighed me down so that I could not move quickly. The dogs surrounded me, circling a wounded prey. But instead of devouring me, they began tearing at the men who guarded me. Moments later, the keeper of the dogs caught up with them and whipped them into order.

"Who is responsible for this?" Tangri shouted at the dogkeeper, who struggled with the string of mad animals.

"The beasts are mine. I will pay for any damages they may have incurred. Be assured the keeper will be punished," came a loud, commanding voice from the crowd.

The dogs were taken away, and a large man dressed in an expensive-looking chuba emerged. Several attendants hovered near, ready to do his bidding.

"Are your men injured?" he asked, glancing at the guards who were attacked by the dogs.

Tangri cast them a look. The men shook their heads. Their thick chubas had protected them from the dogs' fangs.

The rich man nodded his head to one of his men, who handed Tangri a small bag of coins.

"I am Cheung-Dok-Dol. Please accept this gold as a token of my apology. I will see to it that this unfortunate occurrence shall never happen again."

"No harm has been done," Tangri muttered.

Before he left, Cheung-Dok-Dol cast me a long, assessing eye, whispered something to one of his men, and nodded.

We arrived at Drepung the following day and were quartered at one of the monastery's many lodgings. In a perplexing gesture, two of Tangri's aides gave me water and released me from the wooden collar, the chains, and the heads of my beloved and her father. I never saw them again. My body was oiled, and I was given fresh clothing.

For three days, I was well-fed and allowed to rest and regain my strength. On the third day, a tray of sweets was brought in, followed by Tangri and two well-armed guards.

"Have you recovered sufficiently?"

I nodded, suspicious of his true intentions.

"I am pleased to see you in better health." He paced around me as he spoke, his brow furrowed with concern.

"I deeply regret the death of your wife and her father. It was not by my hand that they died."

Breathing deeply, he continued, "I am considering giving you your freedom, Lobnear-Wa."

His hooded eyelids raised lazily as if posing the question, Are you interested?

"Your freedom is yours. I need only to know the truth about one thing. When we were children back at the gompa, you told the old monk about the beatings I gave you and the others, didn't you?"

"I do not understand," I answered.

"It was you who told the old monk of the beatings I gave the others. That is why he withdrew his love from me and showered it upon you, isn't it?" he said anxiously, as if trying to help me remember.

"Tangri, I never did such a thing. I never needed to tell the old monk anything. He knew from looking at your face."

"Liar! You schemed and spoke against me to gain his favor! You caused my struggle for his attention and love, and that is how I became what I am!" he shouted.

A terrible silence closed in upon us. Softly, I spoke with measured words, "You reveal your own true nature, Tangri. Do you think promises of freedom can purify the guilt and anger in your heart?"

Darkness came over his face, as gray clouds cover the sun before a great rain. His hand swept slowly to one side, and in a whipping snakelike motion, he struck my face. At the smacking sound, two guards ran to pin my arms behind my back. Blood streamed down my chin as my numbed lip swelled.

A twisted grimace turned Tangri into the likeness of a demon.

"Fool! I hold your life in my hand! I can flay you alive. I can cut out one of your lungs and hack away half of your face so that you are like me. I could savor your torture over many months—or I could keep you in agony forever. Then we would see whose heart holds more anger!"

Tangri was interrupted by the entrance of one of his aides.

"Forgive me, but the regent of Drepung has a message for you," the aide relayed, his eyes looking nervously down in obeisance.

"What is it?" Tangri fumed.

"The regent has invited you to the festival in the courtyard of the monastery. There will be several officials there, and he requests your presence. I would not have come at such an inopportune moment, but the festival will begin shortly," the aide added quickly.

"Tell him I would be honored to accept," Tangri growled through clenched teeth.

Bowing, the aide left us.

"I will finish with you later!" he menaced. To the two guards holding me, he barked, "Chain him to a pillar in one of the back rooms. When I return, we shall begin by flaying his fingers."

18
Sold as a Slave

At the end of the day, two of Tangri's guards and an expensively dressed stranger entered the room where I stood chained. I steeled myself for the torture, but instead the guards untied me and removed my chains.

"You are fortunate," the stranger whispered to me as the guards took the shackles from my feet. "Cheung-Dok-Dol has taken an interest in you. Come. You now belong to him." The stranger beckoned me to follow him.

As we walked from the monastery and out to the road, he explained, "I am one of Cheung-Dok-Dol's servants. When Cheung-Dok-Dol's dogs did not tear you apart in the streets of Lhasa, he wanted to know more about you. During the festival, he sat with the regent, officials of the governing body of Drepung, and others from important monasteries. The lama Tangri was among them.

"When Cheung-Dok-Dol discovered you were Tangri's prisoner, he offered to donate one hundred gold pieces to Drepung's coffers if he could have you as his slave. Tangri refused, saying you were to be brought to justice. But Cheung-Dok-Dol is one of the most powerful and influential men in Tibet. His friends include the regent to the Dalai Lama and many other high officials in Lhasa and Drepung.

"The regent, of course, showed much interest in the donation and urged Tangri to show mercy and compassion. 'To do so,' he reasoned, 'would be an astute act of diplomacy for a young administrator such as yourself.' Tangri complied, and now I bring you to the house of Cheung-Dok-Dol."

"Why did Cheung-Dok-Dol send only one servant to bring me to his house? Why did he not send guards as well?" I asked suspiciously, well aware that I could easily bolt to freedom.

The servant gave me a knowing smile, "Cheung-Dok-Dol knew you would not try to escape. He makes his livelihood judging men's characters, and he is seldom wrong."

We reached the streets of Lhasa the next day. Within the narrow, crowded walkways, I felt a sudden tingling in my spine, and an uneasiness grew in the pit of my stomach. I tried to discount the feeling, but a silent voice spoke a sharp warning, "Your lives are in danger."

Behind us, I saw three men I remembered from Tangri's entourage. Once they realized I had recognized them, they started toward us, brandishing daggers.

"Someone is following," I said urgently to the servant. "Run!"

"The coins. Use one of the coins," the inner voice called to me.

Without thinking, I reached in the folds of my chuba and found one of my two remaining coins. Running through the crowd, I waved it for all to see and shouted, "A gold coin for the poor!" and threw it high into the air. Before it hit the ground, dozens of beggars who lined the street scrambled for the precious piece of metal, filling the narrow street with chaos. Our pursuers were caught in the middle of the fray while we escaped to a side street.

When we reached the huge estate of Cheung-Dok-Dol, I was fed, given fine clothing to wear, and led to a private room. The servant bowed in my doorway: "Cheung-Dok-Dol will see you when the festival is over in two days. Until then, I shall be honored to furnish all you need."

* * *

"Come in, Lobnear-Wa. My servant has informed me of your escape from assassins. I owe you my thanks for saving not only your own life, but his as well," Cheung-Dok-Dol said as he offered me a seat on a cushion in his spacious drawing room.

He was a large man—rotund, yet imposing. He used his bulk and height to his advantage as a strength, rather than a burden. His face framed deep, penetrating eyes. A long, well-kept mustache and a few long hairs on his chin accentuated the firmness of his jaw. He wore his hair very short—like a monk's—so his scalp shone through.

A servant entered and placed cups of hot, yak-buttered tea on the low table. As we drank the warm, salty brew, Cheung-Dok-Dol stared directly at my eyes for a long moment before speaking.

"Perhaps you wish to know why I purchased you?" he uttered in his deeply powerful but controlled voice.

"As you wish," I returned.

"I first saw you in the streets of Lhasa. I was returning from a hunting expedition. The dogs had broken the chain held by my keeper. These dogs did not attack you, yet they bit those who guarded you. I do not let incidents of this kind go unnoticed," he enunciated carefully, sharpening his stare at me. I said nothing.

"You did not run when all others panicked. There is a fearlessness about you. That is a rare quality."

"My lord, I did not run because I could not. I was chained," I replied, gently.

There was a silence between us, as his face grew sharper. Then suddenly, he let loose a peal of laughter, like a crack of thunder.

"Hah! You would dare tell the truth to me? That is true fearlessness! You see! I was not wrong, after all!"

When he ceased laughing, his cool stare had warmed considerably.

"My friend, you are quite right. But that still does not explain why my dogs did not tear you to pieces. I meet many men, but so very few are truly fearless. That is a rare and respectable quality. When I see such a man, I want to meet him—even if I have to buy him to do so!

"A fearless man is not afraid to see truth. And a man unafraid to see truth can be very valuable to me. Do you have any skills?"

"I know how to farm," I answered, becoming more fascinated with him.

"Bah! Farmers! There are thousands of them. What else?"

"I can cook," I said, remembering my experience in Katsupari's kitchens.

"I have the best cooks in Tibet. What else?" he snapped, impatiently.

"I was raised to be a lama."

"I deal with enough parasites! What else?" he ranted, leaning closer.

"I know how to read and write." I was running out of skills to mention.

"Now we are getting somewhere!" he said, breathing a sigh of relief. I did so as well.

"But I have no need of scholars, for I can read and write myself. I assume you can count then? Keep records?"

"Yes, I can count, and I know how to record numbers," I recalled, remembering some of my duties at the monastery in Thung-yule.

"Then you shall work with my accountants!" he said with finality, folding his arms, satisfied with himself.

"As you wish, my lord."

"We leave on caravan with the spring thaw. We go to the lands of the west. There will be ample time for you to learn the ways of trade before we leave. I shall arrange for others to teach you."

He nodded slightly to me, signaling that I could leave. Bowing, I left his quarters. Another servant waited to take me to my room.

That night, my thoughts pondered the turn of events that had changed my life so quickly in Lhasa. I had been miraculously rescued from Tangri's dungeon, but now I was a slave again—granted, well taken care of, but a slave nonetheless. I desired the freedom to pursue my search for Sri Yaubl Sacabi. A gnawing impatience tore at my heart once again.

19
The Bandit

For nearly a moon cycle, the accountants trained me in their system of record-keeping. I was also taught the names of different cities, monasteries, merchants, princes, and the materials to be bought or sold. I learned a basic history of each city's political, economic, and cultural situations so I would understand their needs, and I was tutored in the language and customs of the foreign cities.

The pay list for the caravan was extensive. Scores of highly skilled merchant traders, animal tenders, agents, and a sizable private army for protection formed the carefully organized group.

The early days of winter arrived, and the initial plans for the spring caravan began. Supply lists were one of the first tasks to be completed by the accountants.

On one day of rest, I decided to walk the compound grounds. Surrounding the estate was a whitewashed stone wall. Guard posts were set along a walkway near the top of the wall. By the main gate, I saw a well-dressed man absorbed in watching the city. I recognized him as Tashi, one of Cheung-Dok-Dol's caravan leaders.

He waved and motioned for me to join him on the rampart walkway. He held a finger to his mouth, indicating that I should do so in silence. When I reached the top of the stairs, he was peering over the wall. Small and lean, his keen eyes darted from side to side. As he watched, he absentmindedly twirled an end of his thin mustache. His delicate hands were finely shaped and manicured. With his pointed facial features and smooth skin, he seemed almost feline.

"The street directly in front of us—do you see the crowd near the cart with the yak? Now look to the roof of the shop directly above the cart. Do you see the young boy there?" he asked in a low voice. "You are about to witness a robbery!"

I saw only two boys arguing loudly in front of a shop. In a burst of action, they began pushing and throwing each other to the ground. The crowd of shoppers soon became a crowd of observers, and a human ring formed around the two combatants.

Tashi half-whispered, "Do you see the youth nearest the yak, wearing the black chuba? Watch him carefully. There are probably three or four others with him, but they are in the crowd and will be difficult to spot."

I watched. Nothing seemed out of the ordinary with this boy, but moments later, one of the combatants was thrown in his direction. The fighter stumbled into the crowd, causing the onlookers to be mildly crushed as they righted him and set him on his feet. Back he flew, into the center of the circle. The boys fought fearfully, and several more times threw one another into the cheering crowd. Moments later, soldiers ran toward the commotion.

As soon as the soldiers were within sight, a loud, shrill whistle sounded from the small boy on the roof.

The combatants scrambled to their feet and disappeared into the crowd. The boy wearing the black chuba left as well, walking steadily in the opposite direction. The boy on the roof climbed down and disappeared into a maze of houses. The soldiers arrived at the scene to find a mass of shoppers wondering where the fighters had gone.

"A very well executed plan," Tashi asserted, nodding his head in admiring approval. "I counted six of them."

"I do not understand."

Laughing softly, he continued, "The two boys fighting were not angry with each other; they merely created a diversion. Each time one of them was shoved into the crowd, they made sure they were pushed in the direction of one of their friends, like the one in the black chuba. The bystanders would take their hands out of their pockets to catch the boy and to keep themselves from falling. In doing so, they took their hands away from their purses, so the boy in the black chuba could take their money. There were at least two others in the crowd that assisted in taking purses.

"The boy on the roof was the lookout. When he saw the soldiers coming, he whistled. This was a prearranged signal that the soldiers would be coming from a certain direction. Many of the spectators paid dearly for their entertainment, don't you think?"

I looked at Tashi with a studied wonder, but he only laughed.

"You must be asking yourself why I concern myself with such matters. You might say it is part of my job. My function with the caravan is to assure its safe passage. I do this by safeguarding against thieves and bandits. That is why I study the ways of such persons, like those boys in the street."

"I understand from Cheung-Dok-Dol that you were a monk," he said, astutely. I nodded. "He requested that I tell you my story. He must trust you and have plans for you."

Eyeing me another moment to assess my reaction, he turned to look over the city. "Very well then. Like yourself, I too was raised in a monastery, though I did not remain. I left because I fought with the temple bully—and won," he said, with a sly grin.

I wondered how such a small man could humiliate a temple bully—a breed I was certainly familiar with. He continued, "After a severe beating from the bully, I allowed him to believe that he would never have trouble from me again. I was merely waiting for my chance. Days later, we were both working in the kitchen. While he held a heavy pot with both hands, I removed his hands from the rest of his body with a cleaver. While he was being attended to, I fled the gompa. Needless to say, that bully never inflicted pain on another in the gompa, but I never benefited from that luxury.

"I learned at an early age that I would never make my way in life through brute strength. Therefore, I had to learn survival through other means. At first it was petty thievery, like those boys you just saw. Then I became the leader of bandits along the roads. Monks were a favorite target, for I understood their ways— plus many of the lamas were rich.

"I prospered by robbing Cheung-Dok-Dol's caravans for many years. He finally called a meeting with me out of exasperation. He is a brave man, for not many men would have agreed to meet with a bandit on his own terms and territory. But that is perhaps what won me over to him.

"In that meeting, he offered me and my small band

something that all the gold we had taken from caravans could not buy: a new start. He offered to employ me as an officer in his trading empire, and the rest of my men could hold positions in his private army. In this way, he eliminated his greatest source of loss and gained his best security against bandits. Who but a bandit could best guard against bandits?

"Before that time, all we could look forward to was life as outsiders—destined to die or lose our hands if caught by soldiers or less benevolent travelers. Cheung-Dok-Dol guaranteed us pardons from the government and monasteries, and lifelong positions if we joined him. Now I own my own estate in the compound. I have a family and am a respected man in Lhasa. Also, I am allowed to keep my attention on the business that I love most: banditry. Only now, I view it from the other side.

"When we plan a caravan, I advise Cheung-Dok-Dol on the safest measures for traveling. Many caravans have met their end because they would not hire sufficient guards to protect themselves.

"The majority of bandits move in small numbers, and a large caravan is too much for them to attempt to rob. Bandits seek self-preservation first, rather than glory or riches. We leave that for military heroes.

"My next area of responsibility is to assure that the caravan does not become complacent, for bandits seek weaknesses as they ply their trade. I have robbed many caravans that believed they were invulnerable or out of harm's way. I never underestimate the strength or cunning of a bandit.

"Harmony is most important for the caravan. Where there is harmony, there is strength, an invisible armor. It is difficult for a bandit to attack and penetrate a caravan that maintains harmony, for its members are at their best. They are alert, and all their attention is focused upon the job at hand. Bandits sense it immediately in attitudes of confidence, single focus of purpose, and contentment.

"I make recommendations to Cheung-Dok-Dol about those caravan members who are ready for more responsibilities. The more responsibility each member has, the more they have a vested interest in the organization's survival. This lifts morale.

"Disharmony, on the other hand, creates holes in the armor, making it easy to rob even the largest of caravans. Disharmony means there is dissatisfaction among the ranks. When adversity appears, no one has the will to defend the caravan. They think only of themselves. And a group that thinks only of the small self, instead of the whole, is weak. Two bandits working as one might scatter one thousand individuals with separate interests. But if a caravan of one thousand thought and acted as one, do you think two bandits could ever take them? Never!"

He smiled and walked toward the stairs. "I shall see more of you, I am sure. For now, I must walk the grounds."

Bowing graciously, he left.

Nothing occurs by coincidence. Was this meeting with Tashi really a lesson from Spirit so that I might learn to steal my freedom? I was torn, for did he not say Cheung-Dok-Dol trusted me? I had never stolen before, but the desire to find Sri Yaubl Sacabi was driving me ruthlessly. I was willing to do anything to find him.

20

Ge-sar

"You are learning quickly, Lobnear-Wa," Cheung-Dok-Dol complimented while visiting the accounting room. "Follow me. There is someone I would like you to meet."

Mounting horses, we rode out of the compound to an open field where one hundred fully armed men on horseback charged at each other in battle formations. Spears bristling, they screamed maniacally. But instead of a terrible collision when they met, they rode through each other's lines. They had just regrouped to repeat the charge, when the low, lonely bleating of a horn sounded. The soldiers raised their spears and trotted their horses peacefully back to the compound stables. We had witnessed the end of a military game.

When they rode past, the last man stopped before us. Cheung-Dok-Dol nodded to him, then spoke to me.

"Lobnear-Wa, this is General Ge-sar, leader of the caravan's guards."

The man nodded perfunctorily but remained silent, looking me over with hard eyes. He was not a tall man, but his thick torso indicated a powerful build. A long scar ran down the middle of his forehead, across the side of his nose, and ended in the thick mass of his black beard. Several smaller scars pocked his cheeks and forehead, and his exposed forearms revealed more thin lines of smooth, hairless skin—scar tissue from numerous cuts and gashes.

"General Ge-sar, Lobnear-Wa is new with the caravan. It would please me if you shared your knowledge with him," Cheung-Dok-Dol said.

"Gladly," Ge-sar replied in a flat monotone, though in fact, he did not look glad at all. He held one expression on his face—one of grim seriousness.

Riding back to the stables behind the rest of the horsemen, General Ge-sar spoke in short, choppy sentences with a low, gravelly voice that matched his looks.

"A fighting man is only as good as his ability to overcome his fear of death. Never fight unless you know you are in the right. Never fight—if you can help it—unless you know you can win. Never be afraid to retreat, but never retreat in panic. Never fight halfway. Fight to win, fight to kill. Never show mercy in battle, but never lust for slaughter. Never underestimate a foe. Never bully another man. Always know that somewhere, there is a better man than you." Staring straight ahead, he fell silent.

Thick clouds of steam billowed from the horses' widened nostrils. For a time, the crunching of snow under their hooves and their heavy breathing was all we heard.

Cheung-Dok-Dol asked General Ge-sar, "If you desire, would you tell once again the story of the pit-fighter? I believe it illustrates the essence of the ideal fighting man."

Ever expressionless, the general kept his steely gaze. "As you wish." And he began his tale.

"Many years ago, in the lands near Samarkand to the west, the tribes of the Mongols were ruled by the ancestors of Timur. During one of the many wars, in which captured nobles were routinely slaughtered, a young boy was spared to fight in the pits.

"The fighters were kept in separate pits two man-lengths deep, with little room to do more than lie on the ground. Food was thrown down to them, and they were treated like animals. They were allowed out of the pits only when they were to fight each other as entertainment at the khan's banquets. They fought in larger pits. Sometimes they were tied to each other and given knives to hack each other to death. Other times, stones or bare hands were used. Life for a pit-fighter was short.

"The owner of this one boy would visit his pit daily, with taunts such as, 'Your parents are dead. I have purchased you like a beast. The only way you may live is to kill those you face in the khan's fights.' Each time a guard came with food or water for him, the boy would vent such fury that they feared to venture too near his pit.

" 'Never have we seen such a savage! See how he spits venom and hate? Why do you not allow him to fight? Surely you would win much money betting on him,' the other pit owners would say. But the owner of the young savage would always say, 'Not yet. He is not yet ready to fight.'

"Each day, the owner visited the boy and taunted him unmercifully. Each day, the boy would fly into a rage. But as the days passed, it would take longer for the boy to fly into a frenzy.

"Finally, the boy became a young man. To pass the time in the pit, he would push himself against the packed-dirt walls, strengthening himself for the fighting he would someday do.

"The time came when nothing the owner said or did would taunt the young man into a rage. Other fighters were shown to him, but while they flew into mad frenzies, wanting to tear his flesh with their teeth, he would not react. He would only look up with a calculating gaze, waiting for a chance to be released. The owner said, 'Now you are ready to fight.'

"The boy was drawn up with a rope and guarded by many soldiers, lest he make a mad dash for escape, but he did not. Instead he was calm, almost docile. When he was brought to the khan's fighting arena, his opponent screamed and frothed at the mouth, but the young man remained calm. When the signal to fight was given, the young man fought with the calm and precision of a warrior of many years, killing his opponent in moments. He fought scores of men, survived, and became deadlier each time. He won because he had learned the secret of controlling himself in the face of rage—not only his opponent's, but also his own.

"The owner became rich from gambling on the young man's victories. However, he knew he would soon no longer be able to profit from him, as numerous wounds would eventually weaken him and spell his end. The young man was given his freedom and a rank in the khan's army. His control of his emotions and anger served him well. In battle, he was able to think, plan, and act with clearness and objectivity of mind. After eleven cycles of service, he rose to become one of the khan's generals. So brave and cunning was he, he was renamed after one of the emperors of the west, Caesar. Thus, the name Ge-sar. I was that boy, the pit-fighter.

"The Golden Horde of the Mongols began to break into three factions. I was given a choice of continuing with my army, but I desired to return to the religion of my youth. Thus, I came to the land of the lamas.

The monasteries would not admit me, saying there was too much blood on my hands. So I have chosen to serve with Cheung-Dok-Dol, doing what the lamas will not do with their own hands—protecting the trade that flows through their monasteries.

"I am not bitter because I am not allowed to worship as they do. It is forbidden for one of their faith to kill. Yet they are willing to pay me to do their killing and protect their money. What life has taught me is this. God will not judge me through an intermediary such as a lama. God will judge me Himself.

"Long ago in the pits, I faced a far more evil foe than any I ever encountered in the khan's fights. That was the anger that lived within myself. Now I can say there is no man that makes me angry, no man I would slay for personal vengeance. I blame no other man for what befalls me, and I have no hatred for another."

We reached the gates of the compound. Cheung-Dok-Dol nodded to Ge-sar, who bowed and rode off to the guard's stables.

"Ge-sar is absolutely trustworthy," Cheung-Dok-Dol said smiling. "There is one other man I would have you meet tomorrow. I will come for you at daybreak." Whipping his horse, he rode off to the compound.

21
Rol-pa'i

The next morning, Cheung-Dok-Dol and I strolled across the estate grounds to a section of the main house I had not seen before. I followed him into a foyer. Thick, flower-patterned carpets from China and carved jade figurines on small wooden pedestals contrasted with the pristine white walls. We were greeted by a servant dressed in red-and-white silk, who seemed to glide on a cloud of impeccable manners.

"Shall I announce you?" the servant asked after bowing.

"There is no need, we shall find our way," Cheung-Dok-Dol answered.

Halfway down a corridor, he opened a door and walked in. I remained outside but glanced in. It was a simply but expensively decorated room. A black stove in the center provided heat, and more Chinese carpets covered the floor. On the walls were several tanned skins, and more were spread over a low table. Near the stove sat a young man, perhaps the same age as me.

"Rol-pa'i," Cheung-Dok-Dol greeted him in a loud voice.

"Father!" the young man beamed, standing up from his floor cushions.

Cheung-Dok-Dol turned, motioning for me to enter the room.

"This is my eldest son, Rol-pa'i," he said proudly.

Bowing, I looked into Rol-pa'i's eyes. They were kind, almost sad. While he did not look weak, his features were soft. His skin was pale—unlike most men in Tibet, who are darkened and leather-faced from the sun which burns intensely through the thin air. His robe was maroon silk, which shimmered delicately, accentuating his sensitivity. He was as tall as his father but had only a portion of his weight and commanding presence. Though we had little in common, I felt an affinity with this young man, and I believe he held similar feelings for me.

"Rol-pa'i is the caravan's navigator. He shall eventually inherit my position. I leave you to learn from him, Lobnear-Wa. Though he is still young, he knows much," Cheung-Dok-Dol said enthusiastically.

As he left, he turned to his son, "Have you finished plans for the route to Kashmir?"

But before Rol-pa'i answered, a wall of tension built between the two men, and their eyes hardened.

"They are complete, Father. But I fear the trade gained in the journey over the Zoji La pass will not justify the risks taken. I believe there is more than enough profit to be made in the lands east of Kashmir."

Cheung-Dok-Dol's lips thinned in a tight grimace as his jaw clenched. "We have discussed this matter before. Do not question your father! We go over Zoji La to Srinagar!" he said impatiently, with a hint of threatening firmness.

"I do not question you as my father. I merely advise as your navigator," Rol-pa'i returned heatedly.

"Then as your superior I say that the final decision is mine! The leader of a caravan cannot be afraid to take risks. You shall never lead this caravan as long as you lack faith and daring!" Cheung-Dok-Dol retorted.

"*I* do not confuse faith and daring with stubbornness!" Rol-pa'i shouted, his emotional reserve snapping.

"Enough!" Cheung-Dok-Dol bellowed, his large, black eyes bulging and his mouth quivering with rage.

Rol-pa'i looked to the ground in silence. Cheung-Dok-Dol stormed out of the room.

The tension in the room fluttered to the ground like leaves falling from a shaken tree. Though we were strangers only moments before, the sudden conflict had exposed a personal side of Rol-pa'i's nature. When we looked into each other's eyes, there was an intimacy and trust that comes with such vulnerable moments.

"Please excuse us. It is not good to quarrel in front of others. Please sit."

Joining me on the plush cushions, he waved his hands over the thick pile of tanned leather skins, with bluish black inscriptions on them.

"These are some of the few existing maps in Tibet. Most have been drawn by Ka-ba, my father's friend and the navigator before me. Before the use of maps, all distances in Tibet were marked only in terms of how long it took to arrive at each destination. Of course, this would vary greatly between travelers and weather conditions.

"Ka-ba measured all of my father's trade routes by having servants count their paces during each leg of the caravan's journey. He was then able to estimate distances and draw maps to all the cities and monasteries. Ka-ba once told me that his goal in making these maps was to give him the viewpoint that the gods had over Tibet—a viewpoint from the high heavens. From this lofty view, distances could be seen as they truly are."

"Ka-ba's last journey was ended three years ago by an avalanche in Zoji La pass on his return from Srinagar. The avalanche swept him and a dozen others over the side of a mountain. My father is determined to return to Srinagar for one reason: to prove to himself that he is not afraid, that he can cross those mountains whenever his will demands. He feels that human willpower and faith can dominate nature. I am afraid he has been lapping up the lies the lamas serve him."

Remembering that I was from a monastery, he paled at these last words and quickly tried to make amends. "Excuse me. Of course not all lamas are liars. I have judged hastily."

I tried to put him at ease. "Please do not apologize. The potential for corruption lives in men's hearts, lamas or not."

Chuckling slightly to cover his embarrassment, he rang a tiny brass bell. Moments later, the servant with the perfect manners bowed in the doorway.

"Some tea please," he requested. The servant bowed again. He returned with two fine porcelain cups and a steaming pot.

Sipping the salty tea, with oily pools of yak butter floating on the surface, Rol-pa'i continued the conversation. "We are entering a new age. I have heard from other traders about a birth of new ideals in the West. But the old ways of our people are not likely to change. Due to the growing consolidation of power by the lamaseries, we are sealing ourselves off from the outer world.

"I have witnessed how the monasteries promote superstition among the common people, saying the lamas are the only ones able to counteract evil spirits. This is only a ploy to further enslave the peasants under the lamas. The lamas already control most of the princes and kings, and are by far the largest landowners.

"With the changes to the east and west the caravan trails of the Silk Route have dried. None but a few small caravans use them anymore. We are the only large caravan that travels them, and so we have a near monopoly on the trade between lamaseries and kings of those lands. This suits the lamas' purposes well, and further isolates Tibet.

"My father is one of the few traders who trades in goods from China, from India in the south, and Kashmir to the west. Because he is half-Chinese and his father lived in the high courts of the Forbidden City in Beijing, he is allowed to travel overland from Tibet to China. The lamas of Drepung allow him to trade in Tibet because he brings needed goods and information from China and the West to the monasteries. He has no aspirations for power—conceding that to the lamas—and so they allow him to become fabulously wealthy. But he is the only merchant they allow such favors. He does not stir the common people, and it is in his interest to keep all other traders out of Tibet as well.

"But I fear this. For one cannot promote ignorance in others without eventually becoming ignorant oneself. I trust and believe in the will of the gods, but I also believe it is the will of the gods that they have given us minds, tools, and maps to find our own way."

As I looked to this young man confiding in me, a plan began to form in my mind. I knew that by befriending him, I would be able to study his maps. When the time came to flee, I would know which routes to use to run from the caravan. But more importantly, these maps might assist me in my search for Agam Des.

He looked into my eyes once again, smiling with trust. But I was not happy. While he had shared his innermost feelings with me, I could only think of the day I would betray his trust and escape. I could not return his guileless smile.

22
A Lost Love

The cold winter months passed quickly in preparation for the caravan's journey. Servants, accountants, and guard-merchants made final checks of the equipment and supplies spread in the courtyard. I was counting barley sacks with the accountants, when Cheung-Dok-Dol paused to speak with me.

"Yesterday I spoke to officials in Drepung. That new lama who brought you here sends a message. Since arriving, his condition has worsened. The physicians say he will not live long. He requests your presence before he dies. Although he guarantees your safety, I will send an armed escort with you lest an attempt is made on your life again."

Allowing his words to sink in, I nodded in agreement. He scrutinized me with a keen eye, then barked orders for three of his guards to escort me to Drepung.

* * *

Tangri's room smelled strongly of pungent herbal remedies and illness. As I entered the room, a physician huddled over Tangri. The three guards searched the room suspiciously with their eyes.

"There is no one else here. You have no need of guards, Lobnear-Wa," Tangri wheezed as he waved off the physician.

"I have little time left before entering the next world. My final words are for you alone."

The physician bowed and left the room. I nodded reassuringly to the guards, who left hesitantly. When we were alone, Tangri resumed, "Before the night arrives, I shall leave this cursed body and begin my journey of the other worlds. Before the dawn arrives, you too shall begin a new life with your caravan. You think you have won our little battle, don't you?"

"There is nothing worth fighting about as far as I am concerned, Tangri," I said with disdain.

"Perhaps, Lobnear-Wa, but as I lay here dying, there is something I have learned that you have not: compassion for those who have lost love."

"How dare you speak to me of lost loves! You—who were responsible for killing my wife and her father! What do you know of compassion? You have always thought only of yourself!" I retorted.

"Yes! And in this manner, perhaps we are not as different as you would like to think!" Tangri said, hacking horribly and gasping for breath.

"Have you ever once put yourself in my place? Years ago, in the gompa at Thung-yule, I was the old monk's favorite. When you arrived, he showered all his love upon you. Am I so different from you or any other man? I needed love as much as anyone. When a man has love taken away, something must replace it. For me, it was love's shadow—power. Of course it was easy for you to disdain me—you had the old monk's love."

"Tangri," I snapped back, "the old monk loved you. You ceased to recognize it. Instead, you chose to hate me."

A sly grin came over Tangri's pallid, sunken face. Instead of returning my sharp words, he seemed to relish them. A luminous glow momentarily flushed color into his misshapen face, like a star that burns brightly before it turns cold. I knew he was dying. Calmly accepting his transition, he ceased wheezing and breathed easily as he quietly spoke.

"Now I have seen and listened to you: still judging, still scorning me. I know something you have not yet seen, but you will. It was easy for me to see. It will not be so for you. Each day has its night. I have just glimpsed the day. Someday you will have to face the night, naked and defenseless without your pride. Perhaps then, you will see me in yourself. Someday, Lobnear-Wa, someday."

He died with his eyes open, staring at me blankly, yet somehow knowingly. Troubled, and not fully understanding his words, I departed.

23
Katmandu

The next day two hundred yaks were loaded, and nearly one hundred and seventy-five caravan members began the journey. The snows were still thick in the Himalayas, but the sun lingered more each day, warming the air. Travel through the passes proved not difficult for the surefooted yaks and horses. Our first destination, Katmandu, Nepal, was thirty days to the south and west. We planned to trade most of the barley grain, yak butter, cheese, and wool from the monastery for goods other traders brought from India.

After passing through the mountains near the holy peak called Chomolungma (Everest) and into Nepal, the lands became much gentler. Emerald green rice paddies terraced the sides of mountains, and trees laden with fruit grew in abundance. Never before had I seen such a land of green lushness.

As we rode single file on a narrow dirt path carved into the side of a river gorge, I looked at the large yaks with their thick, shaggy black coats and long horns. Ordinarily, these beasts were too ill-tempered for me to have compassion for, but I silently thanked them for bearing the loads they did. Each carried more than seven times the weight a strong man could carry over the same distance.

When we arrived on the outskirts of Katmandu, camp was made while Cheung-Dok-Dol, Rol-pa'i, and the other heads of the caravan prepared to enter the old city to find buyers. I was invited to observe and learn more about trading. As we walked through the gates, I was transfixed by the melange of sights, smells, and sounds.

Ancient, darkened, multistoried buildings blocked the sun, forming cramped valleys of streets filled with merchants and shoppers—shouting, bargaining, and hawking their wares. Curry and clove laced the smoke from fires where meats grilled. The smell of baking breads wafted and intermingled with dust and burning incense. The air was warm and humid. This was a great departure from the crisp, dry air of Tibet. The people of Nepal matched the climate: they were dark-skinned and small, with refined, gentle features.

Small temples with carved stone figures and brass gods and goddesses graced the street corners. Holy men in robes, orange paint streaked down their foreheads, chanted or meditated everywhere. Cows, goats, and other animals roamed languidly through the streets, delaying the crowd while children played. In every conceivable space, merchants sold sweetmeats, cakes, breads, pewter, brass, copper pots, knives, tools, bolts of silk and colorful cloths, rugs, and trinkets. In the squares, women spread blankets and covered them with herbs, spices, vegetables, nuts, and exotic fruits that I had never seen before.

For five days we traded in Katmandu. We traded our goods from Drepung for items from India and Nepal. We retraced our way north through the passes and turned west. We headed toward Leh, stopping only to sell goods from Katmandu to the monasteries along the way. More than two moon cycles later, we finally reached the barren outskirts of Leh.

After the camp tents were pitched and the yaks herded, I worked with Rol-pa'i and the accountants to assess our profits.

Flipping through the accounting books, Rol-pa'i nodded his head, deep in thought. Moments later, Cheung-Dok-Dol strode into the accountants' tent.

"What do the numbers tell us?" he asked in a loud, enthusiastic voice.

Gyatso, the head accountant answered, "We have been blessed with good fortune."

Cheung-Dok-Dol nodded approvingly and turned to Rol-pa'i. "What is the condition of Zoji La?"

Rol-pa'i replied, "The pass is clear according to information gathered in the markets of Leh. But if we trade for goods from the west in Leh instead of Srinagar, we would do well enough. Father, the risk of crossing Zoji La may jeopardize all we have earned."

Cheung-Dok-Dol's back and jaw stiffened. "There is more profit to be made in Srinagar. If we do not take risks, we will not survive—this is what our livelihood is based upon. Tomorrow, we shall trade for silver and gold with the surrounding monasteries. We shall not accrue western goods here, but will wait until we reach Srinagar," he said with finality. Before stalking out of the tent, he summoned the full force of his personal power and glared at Rol-pa'i, who remained silent.

24
Zoji La

After trading, we camped at the foot of the mountains, the last flat ground we would see before the long trek through the pass.

That evening, Rol-pa'i called a meeting of the main officials of the caravan. Cheung-Dok-Dol was the last to enter the tent. As he strode in, a stiff silence followed. All eyes turned to Rol-pa'i, who stood and spoke.

"Father, there are many in the camp who do not wish to go over Zoji La. The risk is too great. Will you reconsider?"

Cheung-Dok-Dol's face reddened, and his fists clenched ominously.

"The decision has already been made! The goods have been sold for gold and silver!" Cheung-Dok-Dol fumed, barely controlling his rage.

"The goods from the west can still be bought in Leh if we turn back now," Rol-pa'i countered evenly, returning Cheung-Dok-Dol's dagger-sharp stare.

"And who would wish to return now?" Cheung-Dok-Dol growled in a low, threatening tremor, eyeing each, daring them to oppose him. All looked away or to the ground, squirming visibly—all but Rol-pa'i.

"Father, I take full responsibility for this plan."

Cheung-Dok-Dol exploded in anger, "You do not own this caravan! I am in charge! You shall do as I say!"

"It has always been that way, has it not, Father?" Rol-pa'i countered. "You do not care about the caravan—you only seek to cross Zoji La to conquer the fear in your heart. You know I am right, yet you do not acknowledge me. Even though you profess to give freedom to all under you, you refuse to acknowledge the one who is destined to take your place! Is it because you fear living without power and authority?"

Cheung-Dok-Dol shook with fury, "You dare to shame me? Get out! You are no longer part of this caravan. You are no longer my son. Get out!"

Rol-pa'i turned abruptly to his servants and ordered them to break down the tent, so that they might leave that night. Cheung-Dok-Dol barked an order to me as he stormed out of the tent. "Count out a portion of the gold and silver for him and his servants."

The next morning, I was awakened by shouting in the camp. One of the servants threw open the flap of my tent in a panic, "Rol-pa'i was taken by bandits in the night as he left the caravan's camp. You are to meet with Cheung-Dok-Dol immediately!"

Pulling on my chuba and boots, I hurried to the large black tent. Inside, Ge-sar, Tashi, and several of the head guards and traders huddled around Cheung-Dok-Dol. Raising his hands to silence the murmuring speculations, Cheung-Dok-Dol pointed first to Ge-sar. "Tell what happened," he said, heavily.

"Last night, after Rol-pa'i gathered his tent, belongings, yaks, and servants, he began his trek to Lhasa. This morning, one of Rol-pai's servants returned with a message. As they left Leh, bandits fell upon them. These bandits took Rol-pa'i and the others hostage. In exchange for safe return of Rol-pa'i, we are to leave all the yaks and goods in Zoji La.

"There will be three rocks piled on top of each other in the pass where we are to wait. We have twenty days to reach this place. If we are not there, Rol-pa'i and his servants will be killed."

Cheung-Dok-Dol turned to Tashi. "Do you know how many bandits there might be?"

"No, my lord, but it is certain they are committed to their plan. They will not back down. Failure would spell their doom. For us to do other than as they demand would mean certain death for Rol-pa'i."

"Ge-sar! Can a mounted guard catch them?" Cheung-Dok-Dol demanded.

"They have a night's start on us. Perhaps we could catch them. However, if pursued, they would surely kill Rol-pa'i."

"Then break down the tents. We go to Zoji La!" Cheung-Dok-Dol sighed in a voice both angry and sad.

As I walked back to my tent to gather my belongings, Tashi joined me.

"The bandits are not responsible for this," he murmured in a low voice.

"Anger, impatience, and disharmony caused Rol-pa'i to be abducted. It matters little who was right or wrong. A split in the family allowed negative power to come into the caravan and prey on its weakness."

The caravan wove somberly through valleys for thirteen days, picking gingerly through several small, winding rocky passes before reaching Kargil. There would be no trading here. Instead of profit, we traded time for lives. Another seven days brought us to the middle of Zoji La. In the narrowest part of the pass, we came to three rocks piled one on top of the other.

Ge-sar, at the front of the caravan, called out to Cheung-Dok-Dol that we were approaching the sign.

As Cheung-Dok-Dol rode to the front of the train, a man appeared far ahead on the road and shouted to us. "Do not come any further!"

We could not discern his features, except that he wore a white turban, had a long bow slung across his shoulder, and carried a sword, which glistened in the sun.

"Do you have my son?" Cheung-Dok-Dol demanded.

"We do," the stranger answered. "Are you the caravan chief?"

"I am," Cheung-Dok-Dol returned.

The bandit pointed to Ge-sar and I, then shouted to Cheung-Dok-Dol, "Those two men shall lead the train to us. Choose two other men to drive the rear of the train. Take only some food. Leave your gold with the animals and your weapons as well. All others wait beyond the three stones. Lead the animals to me. When the last of the caravan reaches the stones, have the drivers call out. Only then shall we release your son."

"How do I know you will return my son?" Cheung-Dok-Dol shouted back.

The bandit replied, "You have no choice. Watch!"

As his words echoed, our attention moved to a cliff behind him. Two bandits brought one of Rol-pa'i's servants to the edge and threw him, screaming, into the deep canyon.

Cheung-Dok-Dol looked desperately to us and spoke in a low voice, "If you bring Rol-pa'i back to me alive, you shall each be richly rewarded."

Cheung-Dok-Dol shouted orders to the rest of his men to leave the pack animals and weapons. They were to take only some food with them. Then, walking slowly back to the three stones, he cast us a look of angry exhortation and helplessness.

When the remaining caravan members were well beyond the end of the train, the drivers at the rear shouted ahead to begin leading the animals forward. The deserted caravan snaked its way around the narrow pass in single file, as Cheung-Dok-Dol and his men watched.

It took until dusk before the two men in the rear called out that they had reached the pile of stones. Two bandits appeared on the road ahead of us. Rol-pa'i was with them, his hands tied behind his back.

As we approached, the ground began to rumble. Behind us, brown clouds of dust kicked down the mountain; boulders streamed down its side like water. The bandits had started an avalanche at the rear of the caravan to seal us off. The animals panicked and pushed forward. We watched in horror as the two men at the rear of the train, with several yaks and horses, were carried off the cliff to their doom. The pass was completely blocked.

The two bandits with Rol-pa'i rushed forward to stop the potential stampede of animals. Dismounting so we would not be thrown off, Ge-sar and I held our horses by their reins as they whinnied nervously and stamped their hooves in the dust. The yaks behind them shoved and gored each other with their long horns, bellowing in fright. Rol-pa'i joined us. With cold horror, I realized the three of us were trapped on the side with the bandits.

Ge-sar must have had the same thought. Suddenly, he pulled a short sword from a concealed place in his saddle. The two bandits whipped the lead yaks trying to push their way to us. As they came near, Ge-sar's blade flashed in quick chops, and the two bandits fell.

The rockslide slowed to a trickle, but the animals continued to press forward in panic.

The voices of more bandits could be heard around the bend of the pass. Ge-sar cut Rol-pa'i's bonds, then stripped weapons from the fallen bandits. Rol-pa'i and I tried to calm the frightened animals. A sudden flash of memory from the Records of the Kros at Katsupari opened for me. Cold shivers ran through my body as I realized I was now where the vision had taken place. I knew the only chance for escape would be over the edge of the cliff. Instantly, my mind and heart fought for control of the situation. My heart wanted me to bring Rol-pa'i and Ge-sar over the cliff to safety, but my mind dangled a vision of freedom for only myself.

If I left the other two, I knew they would be killed by the bandits, and I would never be found. Cheung-Dok-Dol would believe I was killed as well. I could elude the bandits and continue my search for Yaubl Sacabi, no longer a slave of Cheung-Dok-Dol. Torn, I hesitated momentarily, but my heart won this battle. Though my mind cursed my actions, I called out, "Follow me, quickly!" and dropped the horses' reins, running to the edge of the cliff.

"No! I die here fighting!" Ge-sar yelled over the chaos.

"Follow me! It is our only chance of survival!" I called back, scrambling over the low, rocky barrier that separated the road from the depths of the canyon.

As I lowered myself carefully over the precarious edge, Rol-pa'i looked to Ge-sar and followed me. Ge-sar soon joined us. The unrestrained animals surged forward on the narrow pass, stirring up a dusty haze. They blocked the road, delaying the bandits' arrival, while providing us precious time to inch down the precipice.

By the time all the animals had passed, it was dark. The full moon rose, providing enough light for our descent. The bandits shouted curses as they searched for us with torches on the road above.

25
The Return

The bandits' faces were red, angry masks, distorted by the wind-blown torch flames, as they continued their search for us. Hugging the side of the canyon, we ceased all movement.

The rumble of a large boulder being rolled came from above us. A helpless, sinking feeling rose in the pit of my stomach. Grunting in unison, the bandits pushed a large boulder over the embankment, just to the right of where we clung. It tumbled like a giant running downhill out of control. Moments later, another boulder bounded and slammed downward, this time further to the right. My body began to shake: partly from the idea of the crushing rocks, and partly from holding on to the side of the canyon for so long without moving.

When the small landslide stopped, I could hear what seemed to be excited arguing. After a silence, another boulder rolled death down the mountainside— this time, directly at us. Clinging to the wall, I prepared myself. Though I feared the crushing boulder, I knew there was nothing I could do. My body ceased shaking. I experienced a surprising calm, perhaps as an animal ceases to struggle against a predator once it knows that to attempt escape is futile.

The mountainside shook once again as the boulder thundered down in skips and bounds, dragging smaller rocks and dust in its wake. The rock ledge I held on to broke, sending me sliding downward. I slid only a short distance.

The bandits shouted at each other, and soon their torches were gone. I put my face in the folds of my chuba to muffle my coughing as I cleared the choking dust from my lungs. Nearby, my two companions did the same. We were covered with dust, but unharmed.

Ge-sar was the first to stand. "They are anxious to divide their loot. They will not return."

Rol-pa'i added, "The mountainside is too steep to climb here. If we go down the canyon, head north and east beyond the landslide, we will eventually reach Kargil."

As we followed Rol-pa'i's lead, Ge-sar gave me a probing look. "When you ran to the edge of the cliff, you could have saved yourself."

Ge-sar was a man of few words. I had never heard him give thanks for anything, perhaps because he felt he deserved whatever came into his life. I knew this quiet acknowledgment was his way of expressing gratitude—or commenting on my foolishness. We walked the remainder of the night in silence.

At the first sign of morning, we came upon the rubble of the first avalanche that had cut off the caravan. Picking our way over the rocks and debris, we found the remains of the yaks that had been swept down the mountainside. To our good fortune, one of them still held sacks of barley and yak butter.

Three days later, we came upon the road to Kargil. In four more days, we arrived in the trading town.

The caravan was not difficult to find, for many of

Cheung-Dok-Dol's men were busy buying supplies, animals, and weapons in the markets. They were preparing to rescue Rol-pa'i. Soon we stood before Cheung-Dok-Dol.

"My son!" he whispered breathlessly, embracing Rol-pa'i as he wept.

"Forgive me, Father," Rol-pa'i cried, but he was cut off by Cheung-Dok-Dol.

"It is *I* who asks forgiveness," Cheung-Dok-Dol began.

"Father—what of the caravan? Has all been lost?"

"I have collected several debts in Kargil to mount your rescue. However, now that you are safe, we can use those funds to purchase goods, refurnish the caravan, and return to Lhasa. We cannot recoup our monetary losses, but we avoided the greatest loss," he beamed, gazing at his son.

Glancing at me, Rol-pa'i said, "Father, Lobnear-Wa and Ge-sar saved my life. The bandits killed the five servants and had no intention of releasing me. They kept me alive only to draw the caravan to them. After the avalanche, they would have killed Lobnear-Wa and Ge-sar as well, had we not escaped."

Cheung-Dok-Dol turned to Ge-sar and me. "When we return to Drepung, both of you shall have your reward, as I promised. Lobnear-Wa, I offer you a share in future caravans. You will be a rich and respected man in Tibet."

"My lord, I have much gratitude in my heart," I stated sincerely. "You once saved my life with one hundred gold pieces. Now I am to receive more for saving your son's life. Since you are a trader, I wish to make a deal with you. My freedom in exchange for the gold."

Cheung-Dok-Dol furrowed his brows in thought.

"I am a man accustomed to getting my own way. Not many men have been able to turn down offers I make them."

To his son, he smiled, "But I have learned much during this journey. I shall never force another to do my bidding. You are free to go, Lobnear-Wa—free to go with my full blessings."

"Thank you, my lord. I shall treasure the moments spent with you and all in the caravan."

"Where will you go from here?" Rol-pa'i asked.

"To the northwest, to the Hindu Kush."

"Is there anything we can offer to assist your journey? Gold? Horses, yaks, goods, food, or an armed escort? It would give me much joy," Cheung-Dok-Dol generously offered.

"Perhaps food—and to study your maps of the mountains."

Cheung-Dok-Dol looked to Rol-pa'i, who nodded in agreement. "I can show you maps of the passes as well as trading villages throughout the Hindu Kush."

"But first, we celebrate your safe return!" Cheung-Dok-Dol boomed, embracing his son again.

26
The Old Man

After departing from Kargil, I followed the Indus river northwest to Gilgit, and then north to the valley of the Hunza. The sparse trading villages yielded little information of Agam Des. Those who had heard of it offered only vague superstitions.

Cold crept steadily into the daylight hours as snow whitened the mountains. I had left the valley of the Hunzas more than a moon cycle ago, passing only small encampments of nomads in the rocky terrain. I traded my labor for food whenever I could and continued to delve further west into the Hindu Kush.

A decision had to be made soon: whether to continue searching the mountains or turn back to warmer lowlands for the winter. I had reached a small river which trickled through a valley between white mountains. The water was low and diverted into many riverlets among gravel beds. Ice formed along the edges of the shallower portions. I was about ready to turn back for the winter, when I saw smoke smudging the blue sky above a hut.

The stone hut was covered with sticks and stood no taller than a man's chest and no longer than three paces. Built beside one of the riverlets, it was a miniature house with one end exposed. An old man in a faded gray robe squatted next to a fire with a small, black kettle over it. A grinding stone spun like a top, powered by the water running by the hut. Looking up, he smiled and tossed a few barley grains on the stone plate. The mill ground them to flour.

"You have traveled far? Come—have some tea."

I stooped to enter the hut and handed him my wooden bowl. I sipped the hot beverage. He nodded and continued to grind flour as he talked.

"You seek a prize, perhaps the greatest prize known to all men. It is attained only by a few. Are you a rich man? Only the very richest can afford it."

"What prize is worth buying if it must be bought with earthly riches?" I said sharply. The single gold coin I had left from my old lama in Thung-yule came to mind.

The old man smiled unwaveringly. "Then you seek riches not of this world? Ah, but then why do you seek at all in this world? Why have you come so far into this barren land?"

"I seek Agam Des," I stated, watching him carefully for a reaction.

"Agam Des. I have been there many times myself. Yes, I know the way—but it cannot be found on any map. It can only be found through the heart."

"I was told it lies in the Hindu Kush," I pressed.

"Yes, it rests there," he conceded, pointing to the snow-covered mountains behind us, "I have seen many who have tried to find it by conquering the wilds. Their bones lie in the mountains, petty bleached monuments to the awesomeness of the goal they attempted to achieve.

"I know the one you seek in Agam Des," he stated quietly, tossing some sticks onto the fire. "The Hairless

One—Sri Yaubl Sacabi. I know many teachers of his line, the Vairagi. I have watched them throughout history. Their teachings are the oldest, and yet in many ways the saddest. Each time they have given knowledge, only a few ever understood.

"But enough talk. You probably wish to be on your way."

"If what you say is true, then there is no need of finding Agam Des and Sri Yaubl Sacabi in the outer world," I debated.

"Perhaps. But goals without outer manifestation are only unfulfilled dreams. Goals without dreams are drudgery. But dreams with outer manifestation become your destiny fulfilled.

"If you arrive at Agam Des, a gift is required to enter. Other than this, the only direction I can give to Agam Des and Yaubl Sacabi is to follow your heart." In silence, his gaze riveted me.

Rising, I bowed. He acknowledged by handing me one of his bags of toasted flour. I reached for the gold coin in my chuba and held it out to him, but he waved it away.

"No, this food is my gift to you. You will need it in the mountains, and the gold coin as well," he smiled. I understood.

Encouraged by meeting the old man, I forged ahead into the mountains, despite the winter cold that awaited me.

* * *

Twenty days later, I had eaten the last of the flour. Travel was slow; at times, my body sank waist-deep into snowdrifts that covered the valley floors. Eventually, I came upon a small encampment of nomads.

I debated whether to use the final gold coin to

purchase grain and butter, or save it for entrance into Agam Des. Intuitively, I felt the city was near. I decided I could go for a number of days without food. I would save the coin as a gift.

Walking around the makeshift encampment of yurts, horses, camels, and yaks, I came upon a dark bundle of clothing. When it moved, I saw it was a young woman huddled shivering in the snow.

"Why do you not seek shelter in the yurts?" I asked her.

As she peered timidly up from her shawl, I could see that her face had been badly disfigured by fire. She clutched a dirty blanket to her bosom, which covered a young child, perhaps one year old.

"I have been left to die," she hopelessly droned, already half-dead from exposure.

"My village was destroyed by bandits. My child and I are the only survivors. I was ravaged and burned by the bandits. Now, no man will have me. I am cursed and unclean. If I had food or money, I could pay my share and stay with these people until the thaw. Then I would be able to reach one of the cities and survive. But I have nothing."

I fingered the gold coin in the fold of my chuba. Against my conscious will, a strong inner impulse overtook me as I withdrew and handed it to her. Simultaneously, a sinking feeling of losing entrance to Agam Des darkened my mind.

"Oh, thank you my lord! A thousand blessings to you! My child thanks you!" she cried, groveling to kiss my feet.

I walked away from the encampment as she gathered her child and stumbled to one of the nearest yurts, her thankful weeping blending with the lonely sighs of the wind as it blew stinging snow through the valley.

27

The Gatekeeper

Twelve days had passed since I had left the nomads. No trail marked my path; I saw only an occasional mountain goat. Night chased the day early in the Hindu Kush mountain range, and I found shelter in a small cave. After pushing snow into the entrance to block the wind, I melted some with my hands to quench my thirst. I was accustomed to fasting for many days at a time but knew I could not continue without food much longer. Soon I would have to return or risk death. I huddled deep in the folds of my chuba and used my training in tumo to warm my body until daylight.

I found myself in the dream world, standing knee-deep in snow, high in a mountain pass. A young man of Afghan descent stood before me, holding a long, wooden staff. His turban and cloak were pure white, and though his legs were bare, the cold did not seem to affect him. Drifts of snow blew from the gray-and-white mountains above us.

"Why do you come here?" he asked, not in words, but in thoughts.

"I seek the city of Agam Des and Sri Yaubl Sacabi," I answered. His cool, gray eyes studied me assessingly.

They were reminiscent of the ancestors of the one called Alexander the Great, who had once tried to conquer the area.

"I am the gatekeeper of Agam Des, the Inaccessible World. To enter Agam Des is a privilege given to a select few. Those who are admitted lead lives that are changed. Great fortunes are theirs.

"It is a law of the universe that nothing is gained without payment of true coin. Therefore, it is required that a gift of the greatest value be given. You have no possessions, is that so?"

"It is as you say, my lord."

"Were you told by the old man at the river that you would need your last coin to enter Agam Des?" he asked.

"What you say is true."

"Yet you gave it away, knowing entrance would be denied without it. Do you think you are exempt from the laws of nature?" he asked softly, but pointedly.

"My lord, I no longer have coins to give, but I do not expect entrance without proper payment. I was told that a gift of the greatest value is given in order to enter. What is of most value to me is not a gold coin, nor a thousand coins, but my very life and my ability to love. I have nothing greater than this."

The young gatekeeper smiled slowly, as if I had correctly answered a sacred riddle. "You may pass. Look for the city not only with your eyes, but also with your heart. It is one day's travel away."

I awoke from a deep sleep. The vision from the night was fresh in my memory. Digging through the snow that sealed me in the small cave, I broke into the morning daylight. The evening's storm had laid a smooth, thick whiteness over the ground. By midday,

I reached the mountains where the gatekeeper had appeared in my dream.

The daylight was intense but ended quickly. The sun descended behind the high mountains, and night claimed the sky with deep blue. The powdery snow that had glistened in the sunlight was now a dull, icy glaze. I began to question that I would ever find Agam Des. Doubt made me weary and the trek more difficult. I stumbled, falling facedown into the snow. My body wanted to rest, but my heart spoke sharply, "Get up! You will not awaken if your eyes close here!" Upon command, my arms pushed my body up. The stinging snow melted on my face and beard, reviving me slightly. Wiping away the icy, dripping moisture, I noticed a warm, golden glow behind a nearby mountain. At first, I thought it was the moon—but the moon was rising from behind me.

Renewed by hope and curiosity, my feet trod toward the light with a will of their own. They broke the smooth blue-white crust. New strength pulsed into my body. I soon reached the base of the mountain from which the strange light shone.

The mountain was steep; little snow clung to its sides. With the full moon's light, I spotted a path to the top.

Over the edge of a sheer cliff shone the source of the golden light. Cold shivers traversed my spine. Partially hidden on a shelf in the mountain was the golden city of Agam Des.

28

Agam Des

The delicate, tranquil air was shattered by the sound of snow crunching behind me. As I whirled to fend off a wild animal or an attacker, a voice called out in my native Tibetan, "Do not be afraid. We are friends."

Three men dressed in thick coats, similar to my chuba, approached. They wore rounded fur hats, which were flat on the top, and heavy leggings of the same material. Each had a sheepskin bag slung over one shoulder. They were of Mongol descent but wore no mustaches or beards. The first man moved slowly so he would not startle me. He pulled his bag off his shoulder. His hand disappeared into the bag and deliberately produced a loaf of brown bread.

"You must be hungry," he said, smiling. He broke off half to offer to me. Cautiously watching each move he made, I accepted but did not eat until he bit into his half-loaf first. The dry, tasty bread chased the tension from my belly and reconnected the senses of my near-delirious mind. When I had finished the bread, the stranger produced a drinking flask.

"We come from Agam Des, to lead you safely into the city." I nodded. I was ready to follow.

We retraced my path a short distance down the mountainside. The leader unhesitatingly picked his way along a narrow footpath and stopped near a small crevice, well-concealed in the rocks. Beyond the waist-high opening, the cave was large enough to stand in. The leader took one of my hands, while I held the hand of the guide behind me. We wound our way along a smooth, dark path.

Eventually, a dim light glimmered in the distance. I assumed the light was the sun and believed it was morning.

"We will rest before continuing," the leader said, pausing to take more food from his shoulder bag. The four of us sat on the cool, dry ground and supped. Later, the others stretched out and closed their eyes to sleep. I thought it strange to stop so short of reaching daylight, but I was tired from the journey. I, too, lay down and slipped into the world of dreams.

In what seemed to be only a few moments, I was awakened by the movements of the three guides. They had changed from their heavy woolen coats and boots to thin white robes and sandals. Their heavy mountain clothes were neatly folded in a corner of the cave. The light of the passageway reflected a golden glow off their skin and robes.

My fatigue was gone, and my body felt lighter, as if I were a child once again.

"Do not be frightened or confused. As we rested, we were prepared to enter the city," the leader explained.

"Are we in the world of dreams?" I asked, remembering the miraculous changes that had occurred at Katsupari from the Physical to the Astral.

"No, we are still of the physical world—but of a different vibration.

"By resting outside the city, our bodies attuned

themselves naturally to its vibration. We changed into lighter clothes for the moderate weather. If you wish, you may wear a similar garment, rather than your heavy chuba," he said, holding out a white robe and sandals for me. The air in the cavern was warmer, and I accepted the clothes.

Nestled into the side of the mountain, the golden city hung over a chasm so deep that clouds hovered below. Tall trees and gardens were scattered amid buildings of many shapes and heights. Warm spring air scented with frangipani and wild clover sent pleasant surges of energy through me. A protective covering separated the city from the harsh elements of the mountains.

Though it was light in Agam Des, stars glimmered in the evening sky. Sporadic red, blue, and green lights streaked and flashed in the darkness to one point in the city, creating a swishing sound as they cut through the air.

"Spaceships from other planets," the leader commented, as we watched the sky.

We descended stairs cut into the side of the cliff and approached the city. I was entranced with the lush trees laden with many fruits. Gardens along parkways were filled with flowers. Berries and melons flourished. Walkways were filled with people of many different races: carrying baskets, riding animals, or moving in strange enclosures. Houses and buildings glowed with many different colored lights.

We came to a hill surrounded by tall trees and dominated by a large, luminous white-domed building. A spacious garden with a long, rectangular pool of water lay before the front entrance. Children laughed and ran to greet us as we walked to the long stairway leading up to the main doors.

At the top of the stairs, a tall, thin, dark-skinned man in a golden robe and turban awaited us. His complexion was translucent, his face was innocent, but his eyes were deep and penetrating. He was a curious mixture of ancient man and young child. He bowed to my companion guides; they returned his bow and left.

"Welcome to the Temple of Golden Wisdom of Gare-Hira. Come." Large wooden doors were swung open from the inside of the temple by two men in knee-length maroon robes. We entered a large, square hall. Dozens of men and women in maroon robes walked purposefully through the hall carrying sheaves of paper, stone tablets, and other objects. They disappeared through different doorways.

My golden-robed guide led me to the farthest corner of the hall. Several individuals were clustered around a stairway. We stopped and waited outside the group. One by one, they departed to other parts of the temple.

I caught a glimpse of who they were waiting to see; it was the one I had searched for so long and hard—Sri Yaubl Sacabi. The breath in my lungs quickly became insufficient. The air surrounding the small group quickened and warmed.

He looked exactly as I had seen him in the world of dreams. Wearing a short maroon robe, he was the same height as me, but stouter. His round head was completely hairless; his skin was tanned and rugged.

At last I stood before him. His eyes were soft and slightly moist, like a baby's. But the force behind his gaze pierced my heart. The aura of his presence caused my body to tingle. Simultaneously, I wanted to laugh and cry from the pure joy of the moment.

When I thought I would burst from his gaze, he turned his eyes away and nodded slightly to my companion in the golden robe. Nodding back, my companion spoke to me, "Come—I will show you your quarters."

The golden-robed monk escorted me through corridors bathed in golden light to a level below the main hall. In various rooms monks worked busily on manuscripts and other projects. We stopped at a room which glowed a pale gold. It was furnished with a bed, floor cushion, and a small, low table. A clear glass pitcher of water, a bowl of oranges, and a small loaf of bread rested on the table. A carved jade vase and three violet flowers graced one corner.

Before my escort left me, he politely said, "If you wish anything else, pull the cord next to your door. I will be pleased to assist you in any manner possible."

I was exhilarated by all I had seen and experienced; but now that I was alone, fatigue crept upon me with numbing peacefulness. I lay on the bed and closed my eyes.

The next morning the memory of my previous life seemed distant and insignificant. After examining the room to reassure myself that I was really here, I pulled the cord next to my door. Moments later, the turbaned monk in the golden robe appeared.

"May I assist you?"

"Would it be possible to meet again with Sri Yaubl Sacabi?" I asked.

"I shall inquire. Please wait here."

Bowing, I remained, while he left down the bright corridors.

It was midday before he returned. He carried a fresh pitcher of water and a bowl of fruit.

"Sri Yaubl Sacabi cannot grant you audience at the moment. If there is any way I might assist you, I am at your service." The golden-robed one's benign smile never left his lips, but his eyes cut deeply into mine.

Disappointment pulled my heart downward, but I refused to be deterred from my goal.

"I have come to learn of God."

"Then come with me," he said.

29
The Cup

The golden-robed monk led me down a quieter corridor to a narrow door. "This room contains a simple map of the worlds of SUGMAD. Each Temple of Golden Wisdom in these worlds houses a volume of the holy book, the Shariyat-Ki-Sugmad."

Windows in the small room let in the sun's golden rays as they poured over the high mountain peaks. The walls were graced with highly detailed and brilliantly colored pictures. Large scrolls with writing in many different languages hung by the illustrations. The golden-robed one pointed to the section nearest the doorway.

"This is a rendering of the planet we reside on: Earth." A blue-and-white sphere floated amid a dark blue background with many stars. "This section of the wall represents the physical worlds. There are many planets besides Earth, many star systems, many universes—but this planet is the only one you need be concerned with for the moment.

"This is the Temple of Golden Wisdom at Katsupari monastery and its abbot, Sri Fubbi Quantz. The paintings of the rolling clouds and lightning represent the sound of the rolling thunder, which is the sound of the physical worlds. The light of this world is the green in the background.

"When the pure Light of ECK enters each world, It strikes particles of matter. These particles change the pure colorless Light into colors. Thus, the lighter the vibration of material, the lighter the color it will reflect. You will notice that there are very few pictures of the higher worlds. This is because there is no matter, and the Light encounters no resistance. It shines clearly in Its purest form.

"In each section, you will find pictures of the various Temples of Golden Wisdom, the sounds and lights of each plane, and the name of the ruler. You may desire to use this room as a map and study guide. If you wish, it would assist us greatly if you translated your understanding of them into your Tibetan language. In this way, you will have the opportunity to serve, while furthering your own learning process." I agreed, and thus began my service and learning in Gare-Hira.

Part of my days were spent in the map room. In contemplation, the golden-robed one would accompany me to the various temples I studied. I would then write down what I had learned, so other Tibetans would have a written guide to these worlds.

In the early evenings, the golden-robed one accompanied me to the Shariyat-Ki-Sugmad, which was in one of the sanctuaries of the temple. There, I read its golden pages.

Most of the time, words proved inadequate to describe my experiences. But by attempting to write them on paper, I gained a more objective viewpoint of the events that had occurred.

One day, after nearly a year had passed, the golden-robed one met me as I walked to the room of maps.

A large group of maroon-robed monks filed out of one of the doorways. The last to leave was Sri Yaubl Sacabi. I had not seen him since that first day when I arrived at the temple.

Once again, my body quickened and warmed. I moved to the wall so he would be able to pass quickly, for he looked intent on reaching his next destination. However, when he saw the golden-robed monk and me, he stopped abruptly.

"Da-lay!" he said enthusiastically.

"Da-lay!" I answered. His vibrant presence startled and enthralled me.

He folded his arms and stroked his chin with one hand while scrutinizing me keenly. Yaubl Sacabi gave the turbaned monk the slightest glance and nod. The tall, golden-robed one quietly left us alone in the hallway.

"I must go to one of the rooms on the other side of the temple. If you wish, we can talk on my way there." Every word carried a quick definiteness. I nodded in agreement.

As we briskly walked, he continued, "The love of SUGMAD is the basis of this monastery, for love is the basis of life itself."

We descended several stairways to the kitchen area. Several workers perked up and smiled at the ECK Master. They continued their chores.

"Not everyone in the monastery eats food from this kitchen. The turbaned one in the golden robe—he is one of the Eshwar-Khanewale, the God-eaters. Long ago, he served as the Living ECK Master, as many of the God-eaters have done. Then, his task was to bring these golden teachings of ECK out into the world to the seekers of truth. Now, he has chosen to serve here in Gare-Hira. After practicing the Ayur Vedha to rejuvenate his body, he partakes only of the ECK Current for nourishment," Sri Yaubl Sacabi said.

He gathered a drinking cup from a rack and a wooden bucket of water. He turned the cup upside down and poured water over the bottom. Water splashed on the table. He then turned the cup right side up, filling it. But he did not stop once it was filled. He continued until water overflowed onto the table.

Amused at my consternation, he rested the bucket on the table. "The water is Divine Spirit, the ECK. The cup is the heart. To receive the gifts of Spirit, the heart must be open. If the heart can only hold one cup's worth of love for Spirit, it is useless to pour two cups' worth into it. First, empty it in order to receive more waters of God's love. The only way to empty it is to give this love to others who are thirsting for it."

Pausing, he asked, "Do you remember when you arrived nearly one year ago?"

I nodded.

"Do you remember your reason for wanting to see me?" he questioned.

The painful memory of rejection was still fresh in my mind as I answered, "I desired your love."

"And what have you learned since then?"

"I have learned that fulfillment does not come by taking love, but by living and giving all for the sake of God."

"Perhaps it is time for you to learn the secret teachings," he expressed sharply. "Come!"

30
Stranglehold

We left the kitchen through a narrow corridor. Sri Yaubl Sacabi spoke as our shadows rippled along the arched walls. "As lovers of God, we are constantly tested: Shall we follow the inner guidance or not? When confronted with an obstacle, most men attempt to overcome it through the force of their wills. In these cases, the lessons of the ECK are rarely learned, for obstacles are placed in life to teach a greater love of Divine Spirit, not how to apply a greater amount of force. These lessons are tests of balance and surrender to Spirit."

At the end of the hallway, we ascended a stairway to the main level. Hushed silence hung over the highly polished, sparkling floors as we traversed the large room. At the end of the spacious room, Sri Yaubl Sacabi disappeared behind a maroon curtain. I followed, but as my hands parted the seam where he had disappeared, I ran into someone. It was not Sri Yaubl Sacabi.

Startled, I stepped back, my fingertips tingling as the blood rushed to my head. I gasped clumsily for air, like a gaping fish, but could only draw shallow breaths. The figure was tall, with golden white hair and eyes the color of the clear blue sky. His powerful body exuded a catlike grace. It was Kotan Runa from Katsupari.

My eyes met his. White panic ran up my belly, cold and uncontrollable. I froze, wanting to recoil. Our locked gaze challenged, then grew narcotically hot and accusing. My breathing became shallow, panicked panting, pulsing with the frantic race of adrenaline. In a flashing move that was as defensive as offensive, our hands shot up to the other's neck in a stranglehold.

Instinct dug my chin close to my chest to protect my neck. His powerful hands shook in a stiff frenzy. The muscles and veins bulged on his forearms as he held me in an angry, viselike death grip. I had to strangle him, before he choked the life out of me. Burning fingernails dug into shoulders and necks, fighting desperately for the throat. His pale white face turned a dark, angry red. The veins in his forehead pulsed. His white teeth bared, he frothed like a rabid dog. His eyes bulged, and the rest of his face contorted horribly. I knew my only chance for survival was to be stronger, more horrible than he.

Grunting, choking, and gurgling noises were interspersed with gasps for precious breath. Our feet shuffled for leverage. Our toes tried vainly to dig indentations into the marble floor. A dull throbbing in my head quickly turned into excruciating pounding, as each spurt of blood strained madly to reach my brain.

My vision of Kotan Runa's crazed face blurred and darkened. In his place, a shimmering figure of light appeared. A familiar warmth touched me through the empty darkness. It was the image of my beloved wife, Shen.

31

I Face My Past

Tears came to my eyes. I yearned to hold her, to look into her shining eyes, to feel her warm breath in my ear.

"Shen! My love. If only there had been a way to save your life. For so long I could not bear to remember you—the pain was too great. Now, I feel this same helplessness once again. If only I could have done more. If only I could have held you one more time and told of my love for you while life was still in your body."

Small tears formed in Shen's eyes as she spoke with compassion.

"Lobnear-Wa, my love, do not cry. There is no need for regret. Please know that wherever we are as Soul I will always love you. I knew you loved me then, and I know you will love me in all the moments to come. I suffered little at death, for death cannot harm Soul. There is no need to punish yourself."

I begged her to stay with me, but her image became translucent, quivering and changing. When the wavering ceased, she had transformed into her father, Lo-tsa-ba.

My heart wrenched with grief as I remembered my friend. "Lo-tsa-ba! Your life would be richer had I not entered it and caused your death. Can you forgive me?" I pleaded.

He flashed a warm, toothy grin, "There is nothing to forgive, Lobnear-Wa. Do you think you are responsible for the choices I made? I am grateful for each moment of my life as it was. If not for you, I would not have had the pleasure and happiness you brought into my life."

As he too faded, I saw the events that led to their deaths on that fateful day. But as I watched the nightmare, I no longer saw it through my narrow memory. No longer did the scenes strike anguish and horror in my heart; I was able to view the circumstances in a dispassionate manner, as if the events occurred to another person.

Sri Yaubl Sacabi's voice spoke through my heart, "You cannot change the events of the past. But you *can* change the way you view your past, and thus change how you see yourself now."

The images of the past wavered and changed once again. Now, I saw the healthy, youthful figure of Tangri, speaking softly to me. I strained to hear his words as they faded in and out.

"We had our differences in the past, Lobnear-Wa, but did we not strengthen each other? You challenged me as much as I challenged you. Perhaps there is no right or wrong, but only lessons to be learned."

His image disappeared, and in its place were the many fights we endured as youths. But this time, I could not view them objectively. My back teeth clenched and my shoulders and neck muscles tensed as I stood before the image of Tangri just before his death, his scarred body gasping for breath.

"What about me, Lobnear-Wa? Can you beg forgiveness for the pain you inflicted upon me?" he hissed.

"I did nothing to you. You received only what you deserved," I argued defensively, clinging tight to my viewpoint.

"Do you remember my words to you as I was dying?" he sputtered, nearly running out of breath. "You were always too good, too pure to be like me. Your physical body just happened to outlast mine this last lifetime; but here, in the timeless realm, you cannot outrun me. The time has come, Lobnear-Wa, to face the ugly, dark side of yourself that you have denied all your life, hiding behind the cheap facade of your self-righteous goal of finding God. It is time to face the demon you have hated all these years!"

As his last words pierced my heart, his arms reached out to strangle me. I attempted to pull his hands away, but he was stronger than his old physical body could have ever been. Instinctively, I reached for his throat, to strangle him before I was killed.

Throttling each other, his face twisted horribly until he began to weaken. But just when his grip began to loosen, his face changed into the crazed face of Kotan Runa once again. I was back in the temple. I had awakened from one nightmare into a worse one. We bore down on one another with every last bit of strength—beyond sanity, into a realm of pure, unfettered will.

When I thought I could fight no more, I felt his grip give, just slightly, but enough to give me an advantage. This heightened the savage instinct within me to survive and kill. I reached some unplumbed depth of strength to finish him off. As I did, he gave up totally, his hands dropped from my neck and fell limply to his sides. His distorted face relaxed and turned white, the crimson fury drained as his eyes closed in a sigh of death. When he opened his eyes again, they were the eyes of my beloved master, Sri Yaubl Sacabi.

Shocked, I released my grip from his throat. His face transformed to my Master's face. Love poured from his gaze, as he calmly opened his hands. Nearly deranged and choking for air from the mad combat, I wept and fell into his arms. He comforted me in an encircling hug. But something was wrong. The embrace was cold. As I looked to his eyes, they changed once more.

A freakish horror paralyzed me. The being was now the filthy naljorpa, with the strength of a hundred men. Wrapping his arms around me, he pinned my arms to my sides and squeezed until I heard my joints pop. Laughing with a sickening glee, his putrid breath made me gag. Lice hopped off his slimy body and onto my face, as the naljorpa savored the moment. I was helpless in his grasp.

He squeezed harder. My breath was forced out, leaving me gasping for air, unable to inhale. Black spots flickered in my eyes. I plummeted toward unconsciousness.

Once more, he squeezed. I gagged on a hot, acidic liquid in my throat. As the thick fluid flooded from my mouth, I felt a mass of tangled, writhing parasites leave my body. The sound of the laughing naljorpa faded away. In the last moment before blackness overtook me, I glimpsed my attacker's face: it was my own.

32
The Greatest Power

"Who am I? What am I?" The impulse ebbed silently. There was no darkness, no light, no space, no emptiness.

It all returned to me, slowly, yet in an instant. I remembered my life and a struggle. Then, the memory ceased. Had I lost the fight? Was I dead? My body was no more. No pain, no feeling. There was no place that I was not, yet I could not identify what my beingness was. A vague longing for home came over me.

I hovered in this suspended state, unsure of the definitions of life. Slowly, I remembered that I had lived many times before, in countless incarnations, both as man and woman. I remembered pain and humiliation, as well as joy and comfort. The constant thread in each life was the search for God.

So many ages, lives, and experiences flashed before me now, as vivid as yesterday.

I remembered the ever-present twins of animalistic existence—fear and hunger. With each successive lifetime, the memories of the past accumulated into instinct. I felt the absolute terror of being torn apart by furious claws, frothing fangs, and the sheer exhilaration of seizing a prey, of lapping its lifeblood. I was the lion and the lamb, the bird fighting the wind for distance, the fish cutting the chilly currents. I was the selfless ant, driven in mechanical armies, and the lone blue whale, supreme in the seas.

Beyond this, I stood above all, indifferent and enduring in the body of a tree. I fought for the nourishing rays of the sun as a plant, and grew in unison as the grass in a meadow.

Nearly timeless, I was the mountain and the rock, and nearly insignificant, I was the grain of sand. Nearly formless, I was the cloud, hugging, yet scattered over the earth. I was the provider of life for a planet, for I was a sun, and again, I was a cool orb, a moon for another planet. I was a star lighting the heavens, I was the darkness of outer space.

I remembered the primal pain: the moment SUGMAD released Soul into the worlds of matter, to live and learn the lessons of beingness. I remembered the sense of separation as I left my home in SUGMAD—a home of light, love, beauty, and happiness—to be cast into worlds of darkness, pain, and fear.

I remembered, and the images ceased.

At first, there was nothing. Gradually, I saw a soft Blue Light; so soft, yet strong enough to illuminate the entire inner universe. With this light came a voice, so tender, I strained to hear. As I listened, I remembered the voice; it had been with me through all my lives, it had been with me forever. So beautiful, so pure and gentle, my heart cried in recognition. It was the voice of my mother cradling me as a child. It was the voice of my first master benevolently instructing me at the gompa in Thung-yule. It was the loving guidance of Sri Fubbi Quantz. It was the voice of Shen, speaking to my heart. It was the voice of Sri Yaubl Sacabi.

In a whisper, it spoke, "Yes, I have been with you forever. I was with you when you were cast from the heavenly worlds. All your many lives, I was with you.

"It was the warmth of SUGMAD's arms you always sought in the arms of a woman. It was the strength of SUGMAD you sought in worldly security. It was the love of SUGMAD you sought in me, the Mahanta.

"Many times our lives have crossed. Many times, you chose to follow, but with each separation, the aching longing would return to haunt you.

"For all eternity you have searched for the Mahanta, the one who holds the key to the greatest force in the universe, the one who could show you the way back home to God."

The beauty was so great, I wanted to answer, but somehow, I was unable to allow the words to come out. In the distance, a slight ripple of white light sinuously worked its way outward from the center. Though its size was nearly insignificant, I felt its motion stirring deep inside me.

Closer it rolled, like a hunter closing in on a trapped animal. I could not move, nor did I have the strength or will to resist. Faster and larger it grew, until it surged, a tidal wave of blinding light. With the rage of ten thousand roaring lions, it crashed furiously through me. My heart and the last vestiges of my small self were ripped apart with the awful finality of a giant oak tree being torn up by its roots in a storm.

With a sound that shocked and awakened every cell in my universe, the fury of the wave washed through me.

* * *

The wave passed. A lonely wail trailed off into a quiet sobbing, a soft trickle of water, like a subsiding tide. The weeping was mine—but the tears were of joy and forgiveness, of compassion and love, for at last the true self I had longed for had embraced me.

I whispered softly. This time, the words came out, "Yes, I desire to love, to give service to all of life."

The voice answered, "Then go. I shall awaken in your heart and consciousness the presence of the Mahanta.

"No power exists that can permanently stop Soul from coming home. This desire to come home is the strongest power of all, and the one who is the Wayshower—the one who never forgets, never falters, and who loves with total compassion—is the guardian of every Soul. The Mahanta waits patiently for all Souls, awaiting recognition so he can guide them home, for the greatest power is the power of love!"

33
The Beginning

I wanted to remain in this sacred presence forever, but it began to fade.

"But where will I go now? What will I do?" I called to the voice.

"You will know me by the Light and Sound. You will know me as I speak through your heart with the language of truth and love. Look for me—I will be there," the voice echoed softly, as though it were far away.

* * *

Though I begged it to stay, the brilliance of the Blue Light began to dim. The sound faded from my inner hearing. From a distance, I heard voices and earth crumbling around me. The white light was becoming larger, yet it was not the pure white light as before; there was a brashness to it. I shivered in a chilling loneliness as I realized the Light and Sound was leaving me.

And now, as though being awakened from a beautiful dream to a cold, uncaring morning, I remembered.

The brash white light came from the hole in the

mtsham. It was enlarged each day by one of the monks who had lowered food and water to me through a shaft in the meditation cave. I was still sealed in, but the opening of the hole meant that my three years was nearly over. Was it all an illusion, a dream?

As the days passed and daylight entered the cave, I struggled vainly to remember everything. But with each passing day, more cloudiness cloaked my memory. My precious recollections of all that transpired scattered like a handful of gold dust blown by desert winds. By the time the opening was large enough to walk through, I had forgotten everything.

I was empty and sad, but grateful to be leaving the cave. Outside, I heard the shuffling of feet. A darkened figure poked his head into my mtsham, and with choppy hand motions, beckoned me to come out.

As I stood near the cave opening, the rays of the morning sun struck my face. Momentarily blinded, I winced and shielded my eyes. Standing poised to step through the opening, I heard the wind rushing outside. The rays of the sun warmed my heart, and a familiar feeling returned. I remembered hearing a Sound and seeing a Light—entranced because I could not trace ITS origins. And suddenly, from the depths of my heart, I knew somehow that the one who held the secret of this Light and Sound would give me the secret to finding the consciousness of . . . no, the *love* of God.

Thus, as I stepped out of the mtsham into the sunlight and the wind, I began the first day of my new life, as Lobnear-Wa, the Seeker.

How to Learn More about ECKANKAR
Religion of the Light and Sound of God

Why are you as important to God as any famous head of state, priest, minister, or saint that ever lived?
- Do you know God's purpose in your life?
- Why does God's Will seem so unpredictable?
- Why do you talk to God, but practice no one religion?

ECKANKAR can show you why special attention from God is neither random nor reserved for the few known saints. But it is for every individual. It is for anyone who opens himself to Divine Spirit, the Light and Sound of God.

People want to know the secrets of life and death. In response to this need Sri Harold Klemp, today's spiritual leader of ECKANKAR, and Paul Twitchell, its modern-day founder, have written a series of monthly discourses that give the Spiritual Exercises of ECK. They can lead Soul in a direct way to God.

Those who wish to study ECKANKAR can receive these special monthly discourses which give clear, simple instructions for the spiritual exercises.

Membership in ECKANKAR Includes

1. Twelve monthly discourses which include information on Soul, the spiritual meaning of dreams, Soul Travel techniques, and ways to establish a personal relationship with Divine Spirit. You may study them alone at home or in a class with others.
2. The *Mystic World,* a quarterly newsletter with a Wisdom Note and articles by the Living ECK Master. In it are also letters and articles from students of ECKANKAR around the world.
3. Special mailings to keep you informed of upcoming ECKANKAR seminars and activities worldwide, new study materials available from ECKANKAR, and more.
4. The opportunity to attend ECK Satsang classes and book discussions with others in your community.
5. Initiation eligibility.
6. Attendance at certain meetings for members of ECKANKAR at ECK seminars.

How to Find Out More

To request membership in ECKANKAR using your credit card (or for a free booklet on membership) call (612) 544-0066, weekdays, between 8 a.m. and 5 p.m., central time. Or write to: ECKANKAR, Att: Information, P.O. Box 27300, Minneapolis, MN 55427 U.S.A.

Introductory Books on ECKANKAR

How to Find God, Mahanta Transcripts, Book 2
Harold Klemp

Learn how to recognize and interpret the guidance each of us is *already receiving* from Divine Spirit in day-to-day events—for inner freedom, love, and guidance from God. The author gives spiritual exercises to uplift physical, emotional, mental, and spiritual health as well as a transforming sound called *HU,* which can be sung for inner upliftment.

The Secret Teachings, Mahanta Transcripts, Book 3
Harold Klemp

If you're interested in the secret, yet practical knowledge of the Vairagi ECK Masters, this book will fascinate and inspire you. Discover how to apply the unique Spiritual Exercises of ECK—dream exercises, visualizations, and Soul Travel methods—to unlock your natural abilities as Soul. Learn how to hear the little-known sounds of God and follow Its Light for practical daily guidance.

ECKANKAR—The Key to Secret Worlds
Paul Twitchell

This introduction to Soul Travel features simple, half-hour spiritual exercises to help you become more aware of yourself as Soul—divine, immortal, and free. You'll learn step-by-step how to unravel the secrets of life from a Soul point of view: your unique destiny or purpose in this life; how to make personal contact with the God Force, Spirit; and the hidden causes at work in your everyday life—all using the ancient art of Soul Travel.

The Tiger's Fang, Paul Twitchell

Paul Twitchell's teacher, Rebazar Tarzs, takes him on a journey through vast worlds of Light and Sound, to sit at the feet of the spiritual Masters. Their conversations bring out the secret of how to draw closer to God—and awaken Soul to Its spiritual destiny. Many have used this book, with its vivid descriptions of heavenly worlds and citizens, to begin their own spiritual adventures.

For fastest service, phone (612) 544-0066 weekdays between 8 a.m. and 5 p.m., central time, to request books using your credit card, or look under **ECKANKAR** in your phone book for an ECKANKAR Center near you. Or write: **ECKANKAR, Att: Information, P.O. Box 27300, Minneapolis, MN 55427 U.S.A.**

There May Be an ECKANKAR Study Group near You

ECKANKAR offers a variety of local and international activities for the spiritual seeker. With hundreds of study groups worldwide, ECKANKAR is near you! Many areas have ECKANKAR Centers where you can browse through the books in a quiet, unpressured environment, talk with others who share an interest in this ancient teaching, and attend beginning discussion classes on how to gain the attributes of Soul: wisdom, power, love, and freedom.

Around the world, ECKANKAR study groups offer special one-day or weekend seminars on the basic teachings of ECKANKAR. Check your phone book under **ECKANKAR**, or call **(612) 544-0066** for membership information and the location of the ECKANKAR Center or study group nearest you. Or write **ECKANKAR, Att: Information, P.O. Box 27300, Minneapolis, MN 55427 U.S.A.**

☐ Please send me information on the nearest ECKANKAR discussion or study group in my area.

☐ Please send me more information about membership in ECKANKAR, which includes a twelve-month spiritual study.

Please type or print clearly   941

Name _____

Street _____ Apt. # _____

City _____ State/Prov. _____

Zip/Postal Code _____ Country _____